About the Author

James S. Catterall is Professor and Chair of the Faculty at the UCLA Graduate School of Education and Information Studies. For the past two decades, his research has focused on measurement of children's cognitive development and motivation in the context of learning in the arts. Professor Catterall has published leading studies on learning music and its effects on spatial intelligence; and studies of learning in the visual arts and the development of creativity, originality, and self-efficacy beliefs. He is now writing a book about the roles of creativity in basic cognitive processes. Professor Catterall's research has been supported by specific grants from the MacArthur Foundation, the President's Council on the Arts and Humanities, the GE Fund, the Ford Foundation, the United States Department of Education, the University of California, the California Policy Seminar, and the American Educational Research Association.

Catterall chaired the National Technical Advisory Panel for the Commonwealth of Kentucky school accountability and assessment system (CATS) between 1998 and 2008; he currently serves as an appointed member of the Advisory Board for California's Public School Assessment and Accountability system and as a member of its Technical Design Group.

Professor Catterall holds degrees with honors in economics from Princeton University and public policy analysis from the University of Minnesota, and a Ph.D. in Education from Stanford University.

Doing Well and Doing Good by Doing Art

A 12-Year National Study of Education In the Visual and Performing Arts

Effects on the Achievements and Values Of Young Adults

James S. Catterall
Professor of Education
University of California at Los Angeles

September 2009

© 2009 by Imagination Group/I-Group Books

Los Angeles, London

i-groupbooks.co.uk

ISBN 1449904335

Printed in the United States of America

First printing: September, 2009

Second Printing: November 2009

Cover pastel by Ms. Robyn Feeley, *bungalowart.com*

Book design by James S. Catterall

Initial funding by the GE Fund

Produced with the Support of The UCLA

Graduate School of Education & Information Studies

Available at *Amazon.com*

Quantity orders reduced cost or free shipping, inquire

i.groupbooks@gmail.com

ISBN-13/EAN 9781449904333

Foreword

The subject of this book will be familiar to readers of our earlier work published in *Champions of Change* and *Critical Links*. Its principal purpose is to track the students we previously assessed over the secondary school years into early adulthood. The result is a 12-year longitudinal study of more than 12,000 students. Our main questions are *Do the Arts Matter, Just How, and for Whom*. We focus on children from low-income families, but report average outcomes for all students as well as similar outcomes for children from high-income families.

Our findings in brief are these: Intensive involvement in the arts during middle and high school associates with higher levels of achievement and college attainment, and also with many indications of pro-social behavior such as voluntarism and political participation. In addition, arts-rich high schools benefit their students in similar patterns. And English language learners benefit from arts-rich schools in unique ways. Then in a specific probe, arts-rich schools are seen to bear characteristics including a climate for achievement as well as instructional practices that may account for their advantages.

This research also goes beyond our first studies to address two pressing questions. Is it *engagement in the arts* that matters? Or is engagement *per se* a crucial factor in the success of our students? The answer to both of these questions is an unambiguous Yes. Chapter 3 performs a unique analysis comparing passionate student involvement in the arts with passionate student involvement in athletics. The results seem clear: involvement in the arts leads to a cluster of important advantages in later life; involvement in sports also benefits secondary school students substantially. But the outcomes differ to some degree. The arts associate with college-going outcomes, certain volunteering activities, and pastimes such as reading books and newspapers. High engagement in sports boosts some achievement and college outcomes. Sports involvement also leads to more volunteering with youth and sports associations, as well as to a life of considerably more athletic activity as adults. Clearly, engagement matters in multiple forms.

We also explore a recent topic of research in the arts and human development. This is the power of arts-rich school environments to enhance the achievements and values of students. While questions surrounding arts-rich schools have been tested in recent years through systematic qualitative research, our database permits an assessment of hundreds of low-income students who enroll in and graduate from such schools. Students who proceed through arts-rich schools have better outcomes in both academic and social arenas than students who attend arts-poor, or arts-barren high schools. We control for family background in making such assessments. *And we take an unprecedented look at students attending arts-rich schools who themselves did not participate much in the arts.* There seems to be a spillover effect on the climate of these schools that works in positive ways. Moreover, the database shows that arts-rich schools are in fact different when it comes to key features of school climate, reported instructional practices, student attendance and social relations, and key assumptions that teachers make about how students learn. This study goes far beyond suggestive descriptions of arts-rich schools. It draws on teacher, administrator, student, and parent data from more than 100 such schools.

Finally, we explore the fortunes of limited English speaking students in arts-rich versus arts-poor high schools. Their adult outcomes are consistent with findings in other domains. English language learners attending arts-rich schools go further academically and bond more firmly to positive social values

This book also presents interesting asides for educators, teachers, and policy professionals. We include a presentation of how the research was funded, the nature of the NELS:88 database and how we developed our indicators, and the basic statistical framework that supported our analyses. And at several turns, we explore the theories that could account for our findings.

In the words of readers:

"Sometimes the solutions to complex problems are hiding in plain sight, but we still fail to see them. There's been a public consensus that our schools are in crisis for over three decades. During that period arts education has been consistently eroded in our schools, the victim of budget cuts and policy makers who are consumed with raising scores on standardized tests. But the schools, especially those serving low-income students, are still in crisis. A decade ago James Catterall sliced and diced data on 25,000 students and found that those who were more engaged in the arts did much better in school and in many other ways as well. Unlike other research on the effects of arts education, Catterall was able to show that low-income students benefited from arts learning even more than more privileged students. This new study picks up the same thread and shows that the positive effects of arts education last well into adulthood. It points directly to a solution that has been hiding in plain sight: our schools will improve if they deliver quality arts education to all students. The students deserve nothing less."

Nick Rabkin

Senior Research Scientist, National Opinion Research Center
Former Senior Program Officer for Arts and Culture
John C. and Catherine T. MacArthur Foundation

iv

"While I'd like to see a concentrated focus on dance education and dance performance in this type of research, a subject that NELS:88 is not equipped to inform, it is refreshing to see the unprecedented comparisons of involvement in the arts with involvement in athletics. The value of furnishing opportunities for adolescents to follow their passions regardless of field may be the overriding point of this book."

Sarah Jean Johnson

UCLA Graduate School of Education
Formerly Modern Dance Choreographer and Performer
University of Oklahoma Modern Repertory Dance Theatre

"I read your book on the train after I left the conference, and it is wonderful. I am going to try to get it ordered in time to use the final weeks of this term in my course on informal learning. The book will show students how someone can make statistical analyses comprehensible for those who work in schools, and, in the case of my class, those who need to think much more theoretically and in terms of research findings, as they curate in museums...

Several of the findings were quite surprising to me, for I had forgotten that the NELS data would provide data with such "long arms" beyond school and family. Such a gift the book will be for so many. I'm ordering a dozen just to send to friends who are always saying "but there's no real hard evidence, is there?" I also want to send it to folks who worked in England under Tony Blair on Creative Partnerships. Thank you, thank you!"

Shirley Brice Heath – Professor Emeritus, Stanford University; Professor, Brown University

v

"In his analysis of involvement in the arts using the NELS:88 database, Professor Catterall does not simply compare students involved in arts to those not involved. He concentrates on students of low socioeconomic status where high arts engagement is less frequent, and where passionate involvement in the visual and performance arts appears to trump economic disadvantage. Set in the contexts of motivation theory as well as theories of cognition and aesthetics, this book was written for teachers, artists in the schools, school officials, and education policy makers".

Jacqueline Bennett

UCLA Graduate School of Education
Formerly University Professors Program, Boston University

vi

Acknowledgements

It takes a village to write a book, even if it's the author who works the 12-hour days toward the end, endlessly chasing after *MS Word* tables that have their own ideas about where they should appear in the manuscript.

I must first thank Linda Johannesen for sparking my conversion to an arts scholar more than 20 years ago, and Andy and Bronya Galef of Los Angeles for their vision and support of *Different Ways of Knowing* at the Galef Institute. *DWoK* became my nursery, *spielraum*, and laboratory. If not for the power and magic of this adventure, I might be nestled today in some club of economists and shunning the real world. I also thank the individuals and institutions that helped launch my arts-related analyses with the *National Educational Longitudinal Survey* (NELS:88) more than ten years ago. These include my daughter, biologist and teacher Lisa Catterall, who helped birth the idea for this project in a casual conversation in 1994. A host of supporters helped realize the work: Jane Polin of the GE Fund, Nick Rabkin and Peter Gerber of the MacArthur Foundation, and Dick Deasy of the Arts Education Partnership who brought me together with the brilliant scholars who eventually produced *Champions of Change: The Impact of the Arts on Learning*, where my early NELS report was published.

I am indebted to Jeffrey Owings, Associate Director of the Institute of Educational Sciences in the United States Department of Education, who helped open the doors of the NELS database, back in a darker age when we mounted ten-pound data tapes on the UCLA mainframe computer. Owings' NELS seminars in Washington D.C. helped advance this work.

I thank Nick Rabkin once more, as well as San Francisco musician Kiff Gallagher, for calling me a year ago to ask if I had followed my art-engaged high school students to the final panels of the NELS survey. I had not. Their encouragement caused me to dust-off the data CDs to take a look at the age-26 profiles. Had interesting things befallen the students I studied a decade earlier? The answer was yes, and I spent the next six months deciding how to frame questions and accumulating a recycled forest's worth of SPSS runs.

I thank UCLA for providing sabbatical time in 2009 permitting my absorption in this project, and for their continuous support of arts-related research at the Graduate School of Education and Information Studies. I also thank our children, Hannah and Grady, for allowing me to work at times when we should have been walking on the beach, attending films and concerts, and enjoying leisurely evenings and weekends together. I thank my wife Rebecca, an educator and ceramics artist, for our 25-year conversation about the arts, children, and society, for her skills and sensibilities in reviewing my writing, and for her smart poking at the ideas and claims in this book. I thank colleagues Sara Jean Johnson and Jacqueline Bennett for their exacting attention to chapter drafts. And I thank California artist Robyn Feeley for her cover design, rendered in pastels after a fun conversation about what the book was trying to say.

Table of Contents

Chapter 1

Déjà vu: Involvement in the arts and
success in secondary school

How the 1999 Champions of Change Report launched this research.[i]

Introduction

This chapter recaps results from our work during the late
1990s exploring interactions between the arts and human
development. These analyses provide the foundation for the
follow-up research reported in later chapters. The main
developments we explored were academic achievement and
the cultivation of positive civic and community values. This
research enlisted the National Educational Longitudinal
Survey (NELS:88),[ii] a panel study which had followed more
than 25,000 students in American secondary schools for four
years at the time of our analyses. The work addressed
developments for children and adolescents over the period
spent between the 8th and 12th grades, i.e. late middle school
through high school.

The first section of this early work examines involvement in
the arts generally--across all disciplines. A second trial
examines the potential importance of sustained involvement in
a single discipline, using instrumental music and the theatre
arts as case examples. We focus on these two arts disciplines
because of related research suggesting links between music
and cognitive development at younger age levels, and in the
second case because of related research on drama and theatre
in education.

Our findings, presented in more detail below, can be
summarized in three main observations:

1

(1) Involvement in the Arts and Academic Success.
Children engaged in the arts show positive academic
developments at each step in the research -- between 8th and
10th grade as well as between 10th and 12th grade. The
comparative gains for arts-involved youngsters generally
become more pronounced over time. Moreover, and carrying
the most importance, this pattern holds for children from low
socioeconomic status (low-SES) backgrounds.[iii]

(2) Music and mathematics achievement. Students who
report consistent high levels of involvement in instrumental
music over the middle and high school years show significantly higher levels of mathematics proficiency by grade 12.
This observation holds both generally and for low-SES
students as a subgroup. Moreover, differences in measured
mathematics proficiency between students consistently
involved in instrumental music, versus students not involved
in music, grow significantly over time.

(3) Theatre arts and human development. Sustained
student involvement in theatre arts (acting in plays and
musicals, participating in drama clubs, and taking acting
lessons) associates with a variety of developments for youth:
gains in reading proficiency, gains in self-concept and
motivation, and higher levels of empathy for others. Our
analyses of theatre arts were undertaken for low-SES youth
only. Our presumption was that more advantaged youngsters
would be more likely to be involved in theatre and drama
because of attendance at more affluent schools and because of
parent ability to afford theatre opportunities in the private or
community sectors. We didn't want to confound the effects of
arts experiences with the effects of student family education
and income levels, and we enlisted specific measures in all of
our analyses to take the influence of SES out of the
comparisons.

We turn now to a more elaborated summary of our first
release of data from this project and then in Chapter 2 to
presentations of observations from our research based on the

full five panels and twelve years of NELS data – extending documentation of our subjects through age 26.

Involvement in the arts and student academic outcomes

In mid 1998 we released a draft study of the effects of involvement in the visual and performing arts on student achievement in middle and high school. Published in the *Americans for the Arts* monograph series as "Involvement in the Arts and Success in Secondary School," this analysis was based on a multi-year survey of more than 25,000 students sponsored by the United States Department of Education.[iv] This study offered the first reported analysis of information in the NELS:88 survey about student participation in the arts. The research used a definition of "involvement in the arts" that gave students credit for taking arts-related classes in or out of school as well as involvement and leadership in school activities such as theatre, band, orchestra, chorus, dance, and the visual arts.

Our analyses found substantial and significant differences in achievement and in important attitudes and behaviors between youth highly involved in the arts and those with little or no arts engagement. In addition--and more significant from a policy standpoint--the achievement differences between high- and low-arts youth were both statistically and substantively significant for economically disadvantaged students. Twenty of the differences favoring arts-involved students were significant at the $p<.001$ level (meaning the odds that the differences were caused by pure chance were smaller than one in one-thousand). Four differences were significant at the $p<.01$ level.

Figure 1.1 shows a number of the key differences we found between students highly involved in the arts and non-involved students, both for all students in the NELS sample and for the low-SES quartile. The figure includes both academic measures and also indicators of students' regard for community service and a measure of their television watching habits.

Figure 1.1 shows consistently more favorable outcomes for students involved in the arts – higher achievement, less dropping out, and better attitudes about school and community. We also see differences in television watching habits, where arts-involved youngsters watch less.

Both our earlier and present work provide evidence that achievement differences favoring youngsters involved in the arts are not simply a matter of parent income and education levels, which do tend to favor children with more visual and performing arts in their lives. Another result, one we spell out in more detail below, is that consistent involvement in the arts shows up in increased advantages for arts-rich youngsters over time, through 10th grade in our first analyses and through 12th grade as well.

A case for the importance of the arts in the academic lives of middle school and early high school students was the primary suggestion of this initial work with NELS. The research did not definitively explain the differences shown, nor was it able to attribute student successes unequivocally to the arts. This caution rises in large part because panel studies are not well suited to unambiguous causal modeling. Nonetheless, the differences were striking, and the chief potential confounding variable, student family background, was reasonably accounted-for in the work.

Introducing theoretical explanations.

There are several theoretical rationales for why the arts could matter in ways suggested. A review article by Darby and Catterall[v] explores much of this ground and points to distinct possibilities. These are grouped into major categories, including the various roles that the arts play in promoting cognitive development--from specific relations such as the influence of music on perception and comprehension in mathematics to the more general roles of imagery and representation in cognition. The arts serve to broaden access to meaning by offering ways of thinking and ways of representation through a spectrum of intelligences scattered unevenly across our population--for example resonating with the multiple and differing intelligences identified by Howard Gardner at Harvard.[vi] The arts have also shown links to student motivation and engagement in school, attitudes that contribute to academic achievement.[vii] Arts activities also can promote community--advancing shared purpose and team spirit required to perform an *ensemble* musical or dramatic

Figure 1.1 Academic and Behavioural Measures, Grades 8 and 10, for All versus Low SES Students, and by High and Low Arts Involvement

	All Students		Low SES Students	
Grade 8 Academic Performance	High Arts	Low Arts	High Arts	Low Arts
Scoring in top 2 quartiles on std. tests	66.8%	42.7%	29.5%	24.5%
Dropping out by grade 10	1.4%	4.8%	6.5%	9.4%
Bored in school half or most of the time	42.2%	48.9%	41.0%	46.0%
Grade 10 Academic Performance				
Scoring in top 2 quartiles, Grade 10 Std. Test Composite	72.5%	45.0%	41.4%	24.9%
Scoring in top 2 quartiles in Reading	70.9%	45.1%	43.8%	28.4%
Scoring in top 2 quartiles in History, Citizenship, Geography	70.9%	46.3%	41.6%	28.6%
Grade 10 Attitudes and Behaviors				
Consider community service important or very important	46.6%	33.9%	49.2%	40.7%
Television watching, weekdays				
percentage watching 1 hour or less	28.2%	15.1%	16.4%	13.3%
percentage watching 1 hour or less	20.6%	34.9%	35.6%	42.0%

work, or to design and paint an urban mural. Or the community formed when students attend to each other and each other's work in individual pursuits such as visual art.[viii] With community may come empathy and general attachment to the larger values of the school and the adult society that high school students will soon join.

James S. Catterall

Learning IN the arts? We do not address here anything
having to do with achievement in the arts *per se*, itself an
important domain apart from any connections between the
arts and more traditional academic or social success. The
NELS database does not contain indicators of achievement in
the arts such as drawing or musical skills--a problem that
should not go unnoticed as future national longitudinal
surveys are planned.

Success by association? Finally, even when looking at
involvement in only grades 8 and 10, the arts show advantages
when it comes to academic achievement in the relationships
we describe, and there is no shortage of plausible reasons
supporting such connections. But even in the absence of
affirmed causal attributions, the perspectives we show elicit
another reason to promote more involvement in the arts for
more youngsters. Our analysis of the NELS:88 survey
established, for the first time in any comprehensive way, that
students involved in the arts are demonstrably doing better in
school than those who are not--for whatever constellation of
reasons. Compendia of research into academic achievement
going back half a century argue that the motivation and
success of one's peers has an influence on how a youngster
does in school.[ix] At very least, our early data support the
contention that when it comes to choosing friends and
activities, rubbing shoulders with arts-involved youngsters in
the middle and high school years is, on average, a smart idea.

> *At very least, our early data support the contention that when it comes
> to choosing friends and activities, rubbing shoulders with arts-involved
> youngsters in the middle and high school years is, on average, a smart
> idea.*

**Extending Analyses of Effects of Involvement in the Arts
through Grade 12**

Grants to the Imagination Group at UCLA from the GE Fund in September of 1997 and December of 1998 supported extensions of this research. There were three general priorities for the continuing work:

One was to extend the analyses describing developments up to grade 10 through the balance of high school and beyond. We were then able to report results through grade 12.

A second priority was to begin to conceptualize involvement in the arts in ways that could capture the potential value of "depth" of involvement. Our earlier work relied on measures of involvement that tended to reward widespread involvement over many artistic pursuits; the most "involved" students in our first study were largely those who attached themselves to multiple disciplines. There are good reasons, however, to believe that intensive involvement in a single discipline would act differently than distributed attention to diverse artistic endeavors. This is because different effects are touted for different arts disciplines, and depth of involvement in one might be expected to intensify particular effects.

A third priority for the research was to explore possible connections between involvement in music and cognitive development. Much interest has been generated by recent studies in neuroscience linking certain types of music training with positive developments in cognitive functioning. We refer here especially to various studies of Gordon Shaw, Frances Rauscher, and others over the past 6 years, described below.

Our first effort to explore the impact of depth of experience in the arts focused on students who reported sustained involvement in instrumental music. Our second effort was to examine students who reported sustained involvement in the theatre arts.

A brief story – finding support for this work –
Or how support found us:

I wrote a draft of Involvement in the Art and Success in Secondary School after spending an uninterrupted week at a computer exploring and running NELS data. I had sensed that something important about the art might lie within and the early results were provocative. I hauled a few copies of this draft to a meeting on arts and technology at the IBM Corporate conference center on the Hudson River, north of Manhattan. This seemed a little silly. People don't read papers at conferences, and the dozen papers they take home are kept unread in a pile for a decade and then recycled. But Linda Johannesen, a long-time colleague, seized a copy as I arrived, read it, and passed in on to Dick Deasy, Executive Director of the Arts Education Partnership in Washington D.C. Deasy approached me the next day and we chatted. On the next and final day of the conference, Dick said that Jane Polin, Comptroller and Senior Program Officer at the GE Fund, would like to meet me. What, another reader? As the final session closed, I found Jane to say, "Hi, I'm supposed to meet you!" Jane responded, "Yes, I'd like to fund your work." And she did.

Involvement in the arts in high school. Before examining outcomes, let's turn to what NELS has to say about the levels and types of student involvement in the arts during high school. Overall, between about one in four and one in six students participate in specific arts forms in a given high school year. Participation is greater at the 10th grade level than in 12th grade. About 23 percent of 10th graders report involvement in band or orchestra as well as in chorus or choir; fewer than 20 percent show involvement in any school musical group by grade 12, as shown in Figure 1.2. Figure 1.2 also shows that the percentages of students taking out-of-school classes in music, art, or dance are much lower than general participation rates to start with, and lesson-taking also declines markedly between grades 10 and 12, especially the drop from more than 11 percent to fewer than 3 percent taking daily out-of-school lessons.

Figure 1.2   Percentages of Students Involved in Arts Related Activities Reported in the NELS:88 Data Base, Grade 12 and Grade 10.

<u>Grade 12</u>   <u>Grade 10</u>

Participates in:

Grade 12		Grade 10	
School Music Group	19.5%	Band or Orchestra	22.7%
School Play/Musical	15.0%	Chorus or Choir	23.3%

<u>Grade 12</u>   <u>Grade 10</u>

Takes out-of-school classes in:

Music, Art, or Dance:		Music, Art, or Dance:	
rarely or never	85.9%	rarely or never:	74.2%
less than 1/week	4.2%	less than 1/week	5.8%
1-2 per week	7.4%	1-2 per week	8.6%
every day or almost	2.5%	every day/almost	11.3%

Socioeconomic Status and Involvement in the Arts

As shown in Figure 1.3 below, we find substantial differences in family income and education levels between our high-arts and low-arts groups. The probability of being "high-arts" remains almost twice as high for students from economically advantaged families, and the probability of low-arts involvement is about twice as high for students from an economically disadvantaged family.

This is why our subsequent analyses of achievement restricted to low-SES students are very important. Not only are low-achievement issues typically more profound for children from families with less education and fewer economic resources, but also high-SES children simply have more opportunities to be involved in the arts, and to benefit from a wide range of supportive resources. When we compare groups by involvement only, the differences are more likely to be caused by differences in family background than anything else.

Figure 1.3   Probability of High- vs. Low-Arts Involvement by Student SES

Probability of high-arts involvement:

      High-SES Quartile .320

      Low-SES Quartile .178

Probability of low-arts involvement:

      High-SES Quartile .197

      Low-SES Quartile .385

Unequal access to arts experiences by family income showed about the same both in the early studies and also after all five data panels were available – but the population from which we drew data differed as the passage of time pared down the NELS sample. We used 8th grade data for more than 25,000 students to gather measures of SES and arts involvement. This means that we had a low-SES sub-sample of about 5000 students to work with, and low- and high-art engagement groups potentially numbering about 500 students initially. This number was reduced when we restricted our early assessments to students who had remained as NELS subjects throughout the three data collection panels from middle and high school. When we took up the analysis at age 26, we wanted subjects for whom we had information at all five age levels in the survey. About 12,000 students met this criterion; about 3000 of these were low-SES students, and just over 300 students showed up in each of our high-arts and low-arts groups. Along with the original 8th graders studied, this newly developed low-SES quartile revealed important information about access to the arts in middle and high school.

Figure 1.4 shows that of the 11,294 students at age 26 for whom we had complete panel data, about 2800 or about 25 percent stood in the lowest income quartile. This group contained more females than males – 1535 to 1239. White students made up about half of the low-income group, with Hispanics, Blacks, American Indian, and Asian-Pacific Islanders accounting for others in descending proportions. The third numerical column in the table begins to tell a story of group economic status in the United States. While only 18 percent of the White students in NELS fell into the low-SES quartile, nearly 50 percent of the Black students and 50 percent of the Hispanic students were low-income by our quartile-based standard. About a third of American Indian students were low income. Asian Pacific Islanders proved to be marginally more well off than the white students – only 16.5 percent were low income.

Figure 1.4 Percentage of Low SES Students Highly Involved in the Arts, by Gender, Race/Ethnicity, Engllish Language Background

Who is Highly Involved in the Arts?	All			Low Income		
	N	N Low Income	Percent in Low Income	N Highly Involved	Percent of Low SES Highly	Under-repre-sented
All Students	11,294	2,774	24.6%	341	12.3%	(< 12.3%)
MALE	5,308	1,239	23.3%	104	8.4%	X
FEMALE	5,986	1,535	25.6%	237	15.4%	
WHITE	7,626	1,374	18.0%	201	14.6%	
BLACK. NON-HISP	1,041	414	39.8%	55	13.3%	
HISP	1,444	711	49.2%	58	8.2%	X
AMERICAN INDIAN	399	131	32.8%	15	11.5%	X
ASIAN PAC ISLANDER	764	126	16.5%	8	6.3%	X
L other than Engl. Spkn. at home	2,568	911	35.5%	74	8.1%	X
R speaks L other than Engl. (b)	1,764	742	42.1%	56	7.5%	X
Highest Income Quartile					39.4%	
Second Income Quartile					25.7%	
Third Income Quartile					23.5%	X
Lowest Income Quartile					14.8%	X

(a) Language other than English spoken at home as of grade 8.
(b) Respondent speaks L other than English at Grade 8.

Arts involvement and SES. The right two columns in the upper sector of Figure 1.4 address arts involvement within these low-income groups -- 12.3 percent of all low-income students were designated high-arts. (Note that we could have ended up with almost any percentage here; 12 percent is an artifact of how we defined arts involvement and where we set the cut-offs for high and low involvement. The standard we used translated roughly to the top and bottom 10 percent of the low-income group, where arts involvement was concerned.) White students, 14.6 percent, and black students, 13.3 percent were modestly overrepresented in the high-arts group. Between 8 and 9 percent of Hispanic students were high-arts students as were about 6 percent of Asian Pacific Islanders, indicating comparative under-representation for these groups. Females showed higher arts engagement in high school than males, by a healthy margin – 15.4 percent to 8.4 percent. *(There are aspects of gender and involvement in the arts that need taking up – left to a future analysis for now.)*

English Language Learners, a designation suggested by indications that a language other than English was spoken at home or the student himself spoke a language other than English, were also underrepresented in the high-arts group. ELLs show as about 8 percent high-arts among a population that was more than 12 percent highly engaged in the arts. *(We devote Chapter 5 to issues surrounding English language status in this study.)*

SES and arts engagement in our full age 26 sample. The lower section of Figure 1.4 shows a fundamental picture of arts education experiences in American society. High-income kids vastly outstrip low-income kids when it comes to opportunities for the arts by a factor approaching 3 to 1. More than 40 percent of secondary students from high-income families become highly engaged in the arts; fewer than 15 percent of poor kids follow in these steps. The second and third quartiles hold their own – they are each a quarter of the population and about a fourth within both groups fall into our high-arts group.

High-income kids vastly outstrip low-income kids when it comes to opportunities for the arts by a factor approaching 3 to 1.

Access to specific arts experiences. This general characterization of access to the arts is reflected in statistics showing engagement in various arts activities documented in the NELS database. Figure 1.5 shows some of these disparities. Participation rates for high-income versus low-income students show large gaps.

Participation favors high-income versus low-income students by 23 percent to 16 percent in band and orchestra, 25 to 20 percent in chorus, and 10 percent to 7 percent in drama. Participation in dance was less associated with income than other disciplines, with about 25 percent of high-income students, and 21 percent of low-income students, studying dance.

Between grade 8 and grade 10, access and overall participation rates were unchanged. Participation in school plays or musicals showed a 2 to 1 disparity in favor of high-income students, and actually taking music, art, or dance lessons outside school favored high-income students by even more. The comparative participation rates depicting high-income, low-income differences are shown in the right column. The statistics typically hover as 50 percent advantages favoring the students in the highest income quartile.

James S. Catterall

Figure 1.5   Access to specific performing arts activities, by Family Income Quartile, Grades 8 and 10.

Percent of students involved in selected arts activities
  by grade level and family income quartile,
  during middle school and early high school.

		Family Income Quartile (Q4 is highest)				Ratio Q4 to Q1
		Q1	Q2	Q3	Q4	
GRADE 8	BAND/ORCH	15.9	22	24.7	22.8	1.4
	CHORUS	19.9	23.6	23.3	24.9	1.3
	DRAMA CLUB	6.6	6.6	7.8	10.2	1.3
	DANCE	21.1	24.9	26.6	24.5	1.2
GRADE 10	BAND/ORCH	14.9	21.2	22	23.6	1.6
	SCHOOL PLAY/MUSCAL	7.1	9.8	11.1	14.1	2.0
	MUSIC, ART, or DANCE class once per week or more.	12.1	17.4	21	26.2	2.2

(degree high income students overrepresented)

High Vs. Low-Arts Involvement and Student Performance.

Our main objective in this phase of this research was to extend 8th and 10th grade analyses through 12th grade. In Figure 1.1 above, we recounted key observed outcome differences between high-and low-arts-involved students as of grades 8 and 10. As seen in Figure 1.6, performance differ-emcees between arts- and non arts-involved students remain about the same across grades 8-12 in nominal terms--showing up typically as 16 to 18 percentage point differences. For example, the percentage of low-arts students scoring in the top half of the standardized test score distribution was 47.5 percent in grade 10, while 65.7 percent of high-arts students performed above the test score median—an 18 percentage point difference at that grade level. At grade 12, the respective figures are 39.3 and 57.4 percent, an 18.1 percentage point difference.

Within the general trends in achievement differences, the relative advantage of involvement in the arts increases over time. This is shown in the relative sizes of the subgroups

14

doing well within the high-arts and non-arts-involved groups respectively, which grow from grade level to grade level. By the 12th grade, the nominal 18-percentage point difference amounts to a 46 percent advantage for the high-arts group. *(This is calculated as 57.4 percent versus 39.3 difference, or , 57.4 / 39.3, which equals 1.46 or a 46 percent advantage.)*

Figure 1.6: Involvement in the Arts and Academic Performance, All Students, by Grade

Percentage in Each Group:	High Involvement	Low Involvement
8th Grade		
Earning mostly A's in English	82.6%	67.2%
In top 2 quartiles on Standardized Tests	67.3%	49.6%
Dropping Out by Grade 10	1.4%	3.7%
Claiming to be bored in school half or more of t	37.9%	45.9%
10th Grade		
In top 2 quartiles on Standardized Tests	65.7%	47.5%
In top 2 quartiles on Reading Tests	64.7%	45.4%
Scoring Level 2 (high) in Reading	61.0%	43.5%
In top 2 quartiles on History, Geog, Citizenship	62.9%	47.4%

Figure 1.7 shows what the comparative achievement advantages for involvement in the arts look like over middle and high school for all students. All group differences are significant at a greater than 99 percent confidence level.

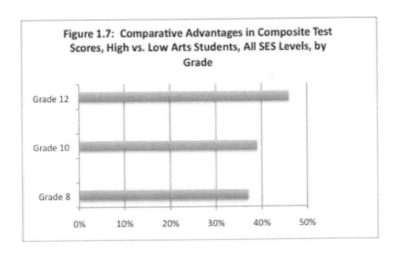

Figure 1.7: Comparative Advantages in Composite Test Scores, High vs. Low Arts Students, All SES Levels, by Grade

This general pattern of increasing advantages shows for various measures in addition to composite test scores – meaning that high-arts youngsters do increasingly better on multiple measures as they pass from grade 8 to grade 12.[x]

As shown in Figure 1.8, the patterns displayed for low-SES students over time bear similarities to those shown for all students. The percentage differences in performance are smaller in nominal terms -- for example 8 to 10 percent lower for test scores. But once again, the relative advantage for arts-involved youngsters climbs over the middle and high school years, and especially between grades 10 and 12. Figure 1.8 illustrates this pattern for composite standardized test scores where the comparative advantage for high arts, low-SES, youngsters is about 32 percent by grade 12.

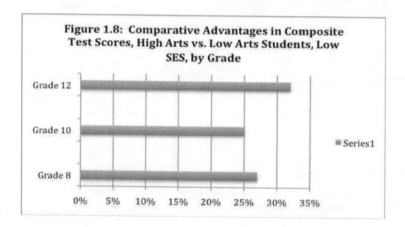

Figure 1.8: Comparative Advantages in Composite Test Scores, High Arts vs. Low Arts Students, Low SES, by Grade

Summing Up

The main conclusions of the analysis are that arts-involved students do better on many measures, their performance advantages grow over time, and that these two general performance comparisons also hold for low-SES children. We turn now to two cases of intensive involvement in specific arts disciplines.

Intensive involvement within an arts discipline: instrumental music and drama/theatre.

Our first monograph adopted a general orientation to involvement in the arts. This was a study of youngsters who exhibit very high levels of involvement within a single arts discipline over the secondary years. The analyses reported above were built on a conception of involvement along the lines, *the more involvement in more domains of art, the higher the student's involvement score.* As such, a student who only participated in an orchestra and took music lessons, no matter how intensively, would not score in the highest reaches of our involvement scale. And looking ahead to our analysis of high school sports engagement in Chapter 3, a tennis player who spent four after-school hours per day practicing would have had no way of scoring as intensively-involved, or high-sports on our scale. We remain hostage to the way NELS selects and poses questions, held hostage but by no means victimized.

Intensive involvement in a single discipline might be thought to be more important developmentally than high levels of more diverse involvement in the arts. If specific art forms act in unique ways on cognition or other human developments, more artistic specialization could lead to deeper impacts. Accumulated research suggests differing impacts for different art domains; so such an assumption seems reasonable.[xi] In general, the argument is that different art forms involve different skills and different sorts of human interaction, not to mention different clusters of resources and interactions in the human brain. In short, different arts impact cognitive processes differently and should be expected to result in different outcomes.

Involvement in instrumental music and cognitive development in mathematics. We address music as an example of disciplinary focus because studies accumulated over the 1990s suggested that certain kinds of musical experiences, especially keyboard training and reading music, and even music listening seem to produce effects on cognitive functioning in young children. One potentially important

17

aspect of the musical experience is learning to read music and
to associate musical notation to issues of time, rhythm, and
pitch. These experiences at first glance appear to involve
forms of mathematical reasoning--the fractional senses of
different musical notes (whole notes, half notes, and so on),
the relative distances of notes within scales and different types
of chords, the perfect doubles and halves in the pitch
frequencies of octaves, and even the relations among dynamics
within a musical passage.   For some instruments, such as the
piano, there is an associated geometry of music that probably
reinforces the spatial, temporal reasoning effects noted by
Rauscher et al.[xii] For other instruments, such as the strings,
there are complex linear geometries, systematically differing
as the player changes position on the fingerboard that are
associated with pitch--that bring spatial reasoning to bear on
the production of musical sounds and phrases.

What research has suggested. While it would appear that
the domains of music and mathematics are widely divergent,
an increasing number of studies focusing on participation in
musical activity and cognitive development in mathematics
suggest that the two are related.   As noted in our introduction
to this section, an important skill developed as a child begins
the study of music is reading musical notation, the symbol
system that represents elements of rhythm and pitch, the
fundamental building blocks of music. It is the analysis of
music at this basic level that reveals the most obvious
connection between music and mathematics. See for example
the Catterall & Rauscher's *Unpacking the Effects of Music on
Intelligence* in the 2008 book, *Neuroscience and Music Pedagogy*.[xiii]
Rhythm, here defined as a pattern of beats occurring over
time, is represented by a series of notes ranging from whole
notes (usually 1 beat per measure) to quarter notes (4 beats
per measure) to eighth, sixteenth and even 32nd and 64th notes.
Two fundamental mathematical skills are consistent with
understanding the time meaning represented in a note: the
ability to count beats, which allows for an understanding of
the absolute value of a note in a measure, and general
fractional or proportional sense, which allows for an
understanding of each note type in relation to others.

A second feature involved in musical notation is pitch or frequency, which denotes cycles per second that define the pitch of individual notes (such as the A, 440 cycles per second, used by modern orchestras to tune all instruments). Pitch differences reflect the relative distances between notes. These relationships in and of themselves are abstract and difficult to conceptualize; playing musical instruments such as the violin, clarinet, or piano helps make these tonal relationships concrete. The keyboard in particular has been singled out in research on spatial-temporal reasoning. The keyboard's layout and its strict mapping to sound are postulated to encourage mathematical understanding. An octave in music is an established, fixed distance between two keys anywhere on the keyboard, e.g. a specific A on the keyboard (440 cycles per second) and the next higher A (880 cycles per second). Or a half step in pitch (F to F#) generally requires a shift in finger position half that of a whole step (F to G). Studies have shown that keyboard training promotes spatial-temporal reasoning skills more than other music study, such as singing lessons. This research suggests that mastering a musical instrument may contribute to mathematical understanding.

Initial studies correlating the grades of secondary school students in music theory and math classes (Bahna-James, 1991) and teacher evaluation of instrumental and scholastic achievement for elementary school students (Klinedinst, 1991) reveal a variety of significant relationships between mathematics achievement and music performance; sight-singing and arithmetic; algebra and geometry; pitch and arithmetic; and finally tonal relationships and arithmetic and algebra. The work by Bahna-James (1991) further showed that the correlation between math grades and music theory grades of secondary school students increases when the mathematics being taught is of a more elementary level and the numerical relationships are simple. Some findings provide additional support for the notion that the fundamental components of music are inherently mathematical in nature.

Research drawing in part from the seminal work of Chase & Simon (1973) on how chess experts visualize and process information, has suggested that cognition in music, mathematics and complex games are activities driven by pattern recognition and manipulation, and as such are affected by spatial-temporal reasoning ability.[xiv] Of particular interest are studies that focus on the effects of keyboard training on the spatial-temporal reasoning of young children as measured by a series of Object Assembly Tasks. These assembly tasks require matching, classifying, and recognizing similarities and relationships among displayed objects. That keyboard training alone (when compared to training in singing or simple arithmetic through the use of computer games) had a significant effect on children's ability to classify and recognize similarities and relationships between objects provides further evidence for the contention that at the most abstract level, music, like mathematics, requires the ability to recognize patterns and relations.

Intentionality vs. Serendipity. We now turn to our basic explorations of differences shown by students who were heavily involved in instrumental music throughout the first three panels of the NELS:88 survey--8th, 10th and 12th grades. We add a word of caution at this point. Some of the studies discussed above were studies of music experiences in their natural state and their associations with mathematics learning. These were generally situations where there was no intention in the music curriculum to bolster math skills; the researchers simply wondered if increased math skills were a serendipitous byproduct of the music experience. Other studies were launched with the explicit intention of producing and tracking connections between learning in the two domains. Both types of studies have found connections between music and mathematics cognition.

Figure 1.9 shows our primary results. We examined the probability that students in different groups--differing mainly by involvement in instrumental music--would attain the highest levels of mathematics proficiency on the 12th grade tests used for the NELS:88 survey. We also differentiated our analyses by family income and education levels.

The results are striking. The overall probability of scoring high in mathematics (that is the probability of such performance among all twenty-thousand plus 12th grade students in the original NELS database) is about 21 percent. These students score at Levels 4 and 5 on the NELS:88 12th grade mathematics test, performance levels indicative of mastery of 11th grade standards in mathematics. From this baseline, the comparisons are distinctive. First, high-SES students on average do better than the average student, an expected result. Second, within groups, students concentrating in instrumental music do substantially better in mathematics than those with no involvement in music. And third, *low-SES students with high involvement in music do better than the average student in attaining high levels of mathematics proficiency.*

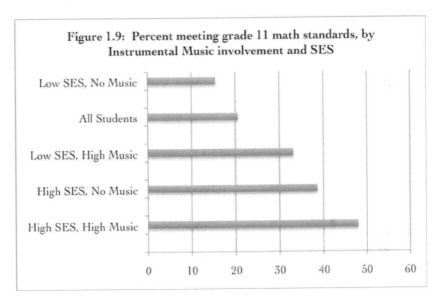

The average high-SES student does better than the average student. Second, within groups, students concentrating in instrumental music do substantially better in mathematics on average than those with no involvement in music. And third, low-SES students with high involvement in music on average do better than the average student at attaining high levels of mathematics proficiency.

Do math skills grow over time with involvement in instrumental music?

The NELS:88 database allows for comparisons over time, and longitudinal growth is an important ingredient of arguments addressing the causes of observed differences between groups. We observed how music-involved students compared with their non-music peers as of 8th grade and revisited the exact same students again in grade 12.

As shown in Figure 1.10, comparisons of 12th grade math performance with 8th grade math performance for the same students, the achievement differential favoring high instrumental music students is much greater at grade 12 than it was at grade 8. The difference is about 10 percentage points in middle school and 20 percentage points during the senior year. Figure 1.10 shows how the performance gaps between the low-SES students involved in music versus low-music/low-SES youth grew considerably over grades 8 to 12.

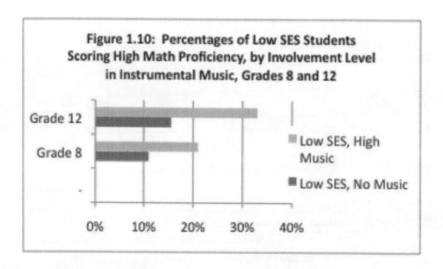

Figure 1.10: Percentages of Low SES Students Scoring High Math Proficiency, by Involvement Level in Instrumental Music, Grades 8 and 12

Involvement in Theatre. Here we explore the results from our original study of the theatre arts in NELS:88. Our interest in the theatre arts grows from a history of scholarship exploring the meaning and importance of theatre and drama in education over the past three decades. The central figures are a number of prominent university researchers in Great Britain. The United Kingdom was the setting for a substantial Theatre in Education (or TIE) movement during this time.[xv] TIE involves theatrical companies taking up residencies of varying duration at schools, usually bringing productions designed to provoke thought and discussion of important themes, as well as to entertain. There are also numerous devotees of "drama in education" in England, including many of the nation's elementary school teachers. This term refers to the use of drama in the classroom for various purposes – learning about history, conflict resolution, learning about oneself, learning stagecraft, learning acting, and so on.[xvi] Drama in education is formally recognized as a curricular tool in the current National Curriculum in Britain, although neither drama nor theatre is a required subject. University teacher education faculties maintain lectureships and even a professorship or two in drama in education, so that teachers in training can learn to use dramatic forms in their classrooms. Britain also boasts a remarkable individual, Dorothy Heathcote, who has become a legendary teacher trainer through a non-stop series of teacher workshops and residencies that have not slowed for 50+ years, even as she entered her mid-80s. Ms. Heathcote advocates that teachers get into roles, along with their students, as they teach. She usually presents her workshops in role to make her points.

In surveying what is known about the impact of theatre and drama on children, Tony Jackson from the University of Manchester identifies "change of understanding" as the general purpose. He goes on to emphasize that the changes of understanding can be about both form and content in theatre. Children learn about the art form as well as about other ends related to personal or social development. Among the latter, Jackson enumerates learning about, "group interaction, discipline, language usage, self esteem, and movement skills."[xvii] Heathcote reminds us also that drama provides situations where we can or must put ourselves into the place of another; thus *empathy for others* is a possible, even likely outcome of the dramatic experience.[xviii]

The strength of research-based evidence for specific impacts of theatre and drama claimed by these and other scholars tends to be weak. Drama and theatre are complex events with many possible effects. What we tend to benefit from most is the accumulation of case studies[xix], along with the informed observations of senior scholars who have been attached to TIE or drama in education and who have come to their own understanding through the gradual acquisition of research and professional knowledge.

In summarizing, we should begin by noting that the theatre in education experiences on which we focus are not strictly those of central interest to scholars of drama and theatre in education. The students in our study identified as intensively involved in theatre are those who had attended a drama class once per week or more as of 8th grade, participated in a drama club as of 8th grade, taken drama coursework in grade 10, and participated in a school play and/or musical in grades 10 and 12 – or at least most of the above. Officers of these organizations were assigned extra "credit" on our intensity of involvement scale.

As such, our drama and theatre students were not necessarily associated with TIE (formal theatre groups in residence on campus) or with drama in education (the use of dramatic forms in the individual classroom for various purposes).

Theatre and language skills. NELS:88 does not contain a measure of spoken language skills, but the data do track the development of reading proficiency in each survey year. We examined the progression of reading skills for two groups of low-SES students beginning in grade 8. One group had no involvement in theatre, and the other group was highly involved in theatre. *(Note: This group is the 285 highest theatre-involved, low-SES students in the entire NELS:88 sample.)*

The patterns in the data are clear. The theatre-involved students outscored the non theatre-involved students in reading as of 8th grade; both groups show higher percentages to be proficient as they proceed through high school; and the advantage favoring students involved in theatre grows steadily to where nearly 20 percent more theatre concentrators than non-involved students are reading at high proficiency by grade 12. The advantage was only 9 percent in grade 8. Students involved in drama and theatre, according to our definition of intensive involvement, spend time reading and learning lines as actors, and may read to carry out research on characters and their settings. More generally, theatre is a language-rich environment and actively engages students with issues of language.

Theatre and self-concept. Because theatre researchers cite self-esteem as a corollary of engagement with drama and theatre, we examined the progression of a general self-concept measure in NELS:88 over grades 8 through 12 and compared our theatre-involved to non-involved low-SES students. Figure 1.11 shows that the "high drama" group maintains a small edge in academic self-concept throughout the longitudinal study. Both groups gain over the four years involved, and a slightly bigger gap favoring those intensively involved in theatre has opened up by grade 12. *(Note: By grade 12, the difference shown in Figure 1.11 approaches significance ($p<.058$).)*

Involvement in theatre and empathy. Dorothy Heathcote reminded us that a dramatic experience is an opportunity to put oneself into another's shoes. This is true when taking on a role; it is also true when, as a character in role, one labors to understand how another character encountered on the stage has conceptualized and enacted his or her role, or to comprehend how others understand his or her own character. Theatre is loaded with potential opportunities to interact with other students, to whom one might not gravitate in the ordinary course of school life, including students from other economic strata and other racial groups. This holds both for interactions among characters in a drama and for interactions between participants in a production as students develop a play or scene or improvisation.

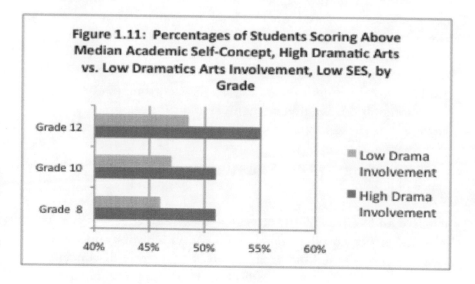

Figure 1.11: Percentages of Students Scoring Above Median Academic Self-Concept, High Dramatic Arts vs. Low Dramatics Arts Involvement, Low SES, by Grade

There are two limited indicators related to "empathy" in NELS:88 and we show results for these indicators on the following pages. Once again, we are comparing low-SES students, one group with no involvement in theatre and the other with high involvement in theatre over all of the high school years.

Race relations. The first indicator is shown in Figure 1.12, and reflects student responses to the question, "Are students friendly with other racial groups?" Students involved in theatre are more likely than all 12th graders to say yes to this question, by 28 to 19 percent. This may be an illustration of an effect of involvement in theatre. It also may be an artifact of unknown differences in schools attended by low-income students where theatre programs are offered. For other unknown reasons, relations among racial groups may be more positive at the schools of our high drama students. This difference is not statistically significant, in part an artifact of the small low-SES, high-theatre sample.

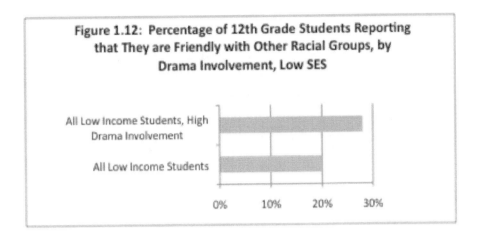

Figure 1.12: Percentage of 12th Grade Students Reporting that They are Friendly with Other Racial Groups, by Drama Involvement, Low SES

A similar perspective is shown in Figure 1.13. Here, students at grade 10 were asked if it was OK to make a racial remark. About 16 percent of non-drama students felt that making such a remark would be OK, where only about 12 percent of "high drama" students thought the same. This small contrast actually amounts to a 40 percent difference between the two groups. The advantage favoring high-theatre students is statistically significant (p<.05).

As with the data bearing on students "getting along" with others of different races (Figure 1.12), what is shown in Figure 1.13 may indicate an effect of involvement in theatre and it may also be influenced by unknown school differences.

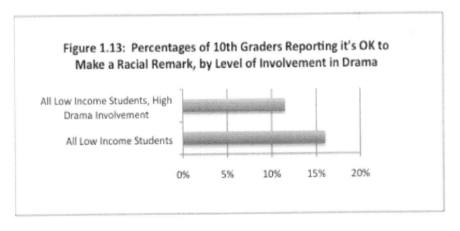

Figure 1.13: Percentages of 10th Graders Reporting it's OK to Make a Racial Remark, by Level of Involvement in Drama

Discussion

The kinds of comparisons and analyses shown above are sure to provoke several kinds of questions surrounding the meaning of the data and the approach we took to examining and displaying the figures. In this concluding section, we attempt to anticipate some of these questions and also to suggest the implications of what we report.

What can be said about causation in this analysis?

Establishing causation in education and social science research presents challenges. The essential question that should be aimed at this type of work is *what evidence supports contentions that involvement in the arts, or music, or theatre "caused" the differences in groups reported above?*

Any convictions that causation is involved depend mainly on three elements of the research – sound theory, supportive evidence, and fair consideration of rival explanations. First is the presence of a sound theory consistent with explanations that the arts should matter. In the case of all three of our analyses, our instincts arose out of previous research suggestive of causal propositions. The strength of the case is perhaps most apparent in the instance of music and mathematics-related cognitive development. Incidental benefits of theatre have been argued and studied for decades. The general effects of broad involvement in the arts are supported most by research that has shown that children are more engaged and cognitively involved in school when the arts are part of, or integrated into, the curriculum.[xx]

A second element is observational data supporting the causal theory. If one cannot find an empirically validated association between participation in the arts and specific outcomes, it is difficult to argue that the arts are causing anything. A version of this argument is that one cannot support causation without significant correlation. Our data point to correlations between arts participation and various outcomes, many quite strong.

The third element is success in ruling out rival hypotheses. We pursued this in several ways. One is by constructing comparison groups to be as similar as possible, with the only difference between groups being, in our case, level of arts participation. We approached this by restricting our groups to low-SES students, so that differences in family background would not drive observed outcome differences. We also downsized rival hypotheses by observing changes over time for the same students. In all three sections of the work (general arts involvement, music, and theatre), advantages favoring arts-involved students appear in many cases to grow over time. A rival hypothesis we have not ruled out is that, systematically, more arts-involved students attended more effective schools in middle and high school. To consider this a preemptive explanation would require that this "better school" explanation held for all three of our main comparison frames, which were essentially constructed differently and involved different students and different schools.

Selection bias. A hidden factor challenges the causal interpretations offered in this analysis, namely selection bias. Possibilities of selection bias by students or their families at least suggest cautions in of the degree of causality we can claim. This term refers to the fact that although we equate experimental and comparison groups on the crucial issue of family education or SES, some families and students choose engagement in the arts for reasons that are unknown. These selection processes can involve acts of choosing activities for one's children and students choosing activities for themselves. These choices may indicate a preferred condition – perhaps high caring, keen awareness of child needs, active parent-engagement in education, or longstanding interest on the part of the student -- a number of possibilities that may help cause participating youth to do better than non-participating youth. But there are no ready ways to measure this factor or to separate selection effects from the effects of actual participation. But, and this is an important qualification, as we discuss in Chapter 3, selection into preferred activities should be considered a good thing, and providing opportunities for students seeking the visual and performing arts as well as other interests would maximize returns from our schools.

Level of engagement per se. It is possible and even likely that being engaged with passion and intensity in any activity during secondary school would have beneficial effects. We examine a challenge to our suggestion that "it's the arts that matter" in Chapter 3, where we look at sports engagement in high school and draw various comparisons of the effects of high involvement in athletics to high involvement in the arts.

Implications

The arts and student development. This chapter presents observations from a large-scale database of U.S. secondary school students suggesting positive associations between involvement in various arts and academic and social outcomes. Our analyses support strong suggestions. No one study ever decides issues in this sort of research. Our knowledge base grows incrementally with the accumulation of consistent studies, and with the accumulation of professional knowledge by educators, school leaders, parents, students, and in this case, artists involved in the schools.[xxi]

The main implication of this work is that the arts appear to matter when it comes to a variety of non-arts outcomes, some of them intended and some not. The advantages stemming from arts involvement show up both through general high levels of participation across the arts, as well as through involvement in specific art forms such as instrumental music and theatre.

Equality of access to the arts. Although not the main theme of this chapter, our data support long-held concerns that access to the arts is inequitably distributed in our society. Students from poor and less educated families are much more likely to record low levels of participation in the arts during the middle and high school years; affluent youngsters are much more likely to show high, rather than low engagement in the arts. If our analysis is reasonable, the arts *do* matter--not only as worthwhile experiences in their own right for reasons not addressed here, but also as instruments of cognitive growth and development and as agents of motivation for school success. In this light, unfair access to the arts for our children brings consequences of major importance to our society.

Strengthening future research. Finally, this work also suggests the value of more up-close and more controlled research that can further test our findings. Traditionally, the strongest research approach is the use of randomized studies. But random assignment to involvement in the arts is problematic when the issue is long-term, natural engagement with the arts--the topic this chapter is concerned with. Also, long-term deprivation in the arts, implied when enlisting purposeful control groups to study the importance of the arts, is probably unethical and could be considered potentially harmful to children. In this matter, we reserve comment on the generally deprived conditions surrounding arts education in today's schools.

Productive approaches to future research might include better measures of the quality and qualities of engagements in the arts. We'd like to know not only that a student played in the orchestra, or joined the dance troupe – but also how truly engaged that student is with these activities. And what learning IN the arts has taken place. Survey research could improve on NELS measures by asking questions about depth and meaning of arts experiences. Research should also include phenomenological studies that probe the meanings of art experiences to individual children or educators. Studies may include up-close longitudinal studies of students heavily involved in music or theatre (or other art disciplines) at the single or multiple-school level to explore changes over time. Studies should be aimed at school-level or larger scale studies of initiatives attempting to bring arts integration to the curriculum.[xxii] Many forms of research in these areas can exhibit strengths, but all will succumb to certain weaknesses and limitations. Knowledge will come at the intersection of multiple and diverse studies of what the arts mean for human development.

Chapter 2

Arts-Involved Students: *Doing well* and *doing good* through Age 26

Our high school analysis grows up. How these kids turned out.

Secondary school years. The NELS:88 survey began with the 8th, 10th, and 12th grade data collection panels. By the mid 1990s, hundreds if not thousands of academic research studies had been published using data from the NELS project. The database contained more than 1000 pieces of information about each participant concerning most conceivable arenas of participation in academic, social, and family life. The successive panels permit measurement of change in student status and student achievement, and provide a wealth of information about the school and community settings and contexts and individual dispositions that may have contributed to growth or change over time.

Predictably, most NELS-based studies focus on the bread and butter subjects of education research. These include language development, along with achievement in mathematics, science, and history. The data permit fine-tuned assessments of instructional strategies and classroom organization, the influence of teacher characteristics and beliefs, the effects of community conditions, peer effects on learning and behavior, and parent involvement in school. The data have supported numerious studies of school dropouts, issues of student risk, and transitions from middle to high school. Name an important contemporary area of inquiry in learning and development and it is possible to craft at least some way of informing the subject using the NELS database.[xxiii]

Postsecondary school years. The final two follow-up data collection panels took place when the original subjects were age 20 and age 26. At age 20, the NELS subjects were two-years out of high school. A majority were pursuing some sort

33

of postsecondary training ranging from trade schools to four-year colleges. More than half of the original subjects were in the workforce part- or full-time by this age.

At age 26, the NELS subjects were eight years beyond high school. About 30 percent of the subjects in the age 26 survey had finished 4-year college degrees. A majority of all subjects held full-time jobs by age 26, and a significant subgroup aspired to finish BA degrees or accomplish masters level or other graduate degrees by their 30th birthdays.

The data collected beyond high school support inquiries into student transitions from high school to college and student entry into the workforce. College selection, deciding majors for college studies, programs in public and private two-year colleges, transfer processes between junior colleges and four-year colleges are all natural targets of study. Scholars have found the influences of family and mentors on these processes to be crucial, and the social determinants of transitions to adulthood appear prominently in the NELS-based literature.

Most important for this and many other studies, the age 20 and 26 data panels afforded opportunities to assess the longer-term effects of events and conditions that impacted individuals many years in the past.

Of the original 25,000 students in the NELS study, just over 12,000 participated in all five panels of the survey. To say that the project's success in tracking down its subjects over the full span of the survey is awe-inspiring is something of an understatement. No single researcher or consortium of scholars could undertake an enterprise as such as NELS; the total budget for NEL:88 was in the tens of millions of dollars. Most published research studies in learning and development present humble apologies for their failure to assess anything beyond immediate or near-term effects.

The arts and NELS' third and fourth follow-up surveys – ages 20 and 26.

Our earlier work with art and NELS described in Chapter 1 assembled information about student participation in the visual and performing arts during middle and high school to identify students heavily engaged in the arts, as well as to identify students largely lacking participation in the arts during the same grade levels. The analysis compared arts-involved versus non-arts-involved students as of the spring of 12th grade. In this chapter, we extend the student outcome comparisons to ages 20 and 26.

While Chapter 6 pursues at some length theoretical reasons why we might expect certain long term developments for adolescents to be influenced by participation and learning in the arts, it may be useful to review the basic reasoning structure here. Arguments that engagement in the arts may confer long-term academic or social benefits to secondary school students include:

1) **Direct curriculum effects.** Research in the arts has showed effects of specific arts pursuits on learning in closely allied curricular areas – for example, achievement in language and reading associated with involvement in drama and theatre. Achievement gains in language during high school would probably translate to added success in postsecondary education.

2) **Educationally relevent neurological development and transfer.** Evidence continues to mount supporting claims that experience tends to rewire the brain and that a rewired brain may perform tasks differently and perhaps more effectively or more efficiently. A clear example has been research in music learning, which concludes that under some conditions, music experience promotes spatial reasoning skills. Spatial reasoning skills in turn have documented connections to language development, mathematics proficiency, and to a broad class of skills identified by standardized tests of intelligence.[xxiv] The critical idea is that neurofunction

enhanced by one experience might provide neuroprocessing capacities that benefit largely different functions – skills that may contribute to academic or social success.

3) Effects of arts learning on motivation. A third body of ideas suggesting that learning in the arts may produce learning in non-arts areas derives from theories of achievement motivation. Important among these is the power of successful learning to cultivate feelings of competence or agency. Specific feelings of competence may lead to optimism and success in other domains. The arts appear to be places where most young children will experience at least some progression of skills in the early years that could produce a reinforcing sense of worth and accomplishment. This may be especially important for children who feel excluded from the regular classroom for various possible reasons – e.g. under-developed English language or social skills.

4) Arts, access to knowledge, and expressive capacity. Gardner's theories of multiple intelligences have been regarded by educators to imply that different children may benefit from different ways of understanding and communicating experiences – through linguistic, visual, kinesthetic, mathematical, and interpersonal forms, for example. So including visual art, or movement, or theatre or dance in academic curriculum experiences may provide children with access to subject matter and ways of thinking, children who might otherwise be shortchanged in a classroom dominated by language-centered or didactic methods of instruction.

5) Gains in social skills and self-understanding that may impact achievement and the development of values. Many pursuits in the arts are collaborative, involving joint effort and cooperation among performers or participants. Music ensembles, dance teams, class mural projects, and acting troupes clearly exhibit these qualities. We assume that abilities to cooperate gained in collaborative art endeavors may transfer to non-art situations where collaboration promotes success.

Cooperation and collaboration produce microcosms of social systems – systems in which goals, visions, and individual roles are negotiated by members. Responsibilities may be shared or divided up and sometimes given to designated leaders or representatives to help articulate and manage. Skills in promoting or participating in the collaborative pursuit of goals will impact myriad academic and social situations where individuals must cooperate to succeed.

5) Play versus the real world. In encouraging play, the arts promote learning about real issues – the way things work, the way they look, the way they could work and look, the consequences of social action or inaction, and trying on the *possible* for size. Learning and development through play-based experimentation almost certainly contributes to success later on -- success in making life decisions, in planning courses of action, and in separating fact from fancy in appraising the dimensions of problems and opportunities. And play is recognized widely, by teachers, parents, the kids, and great scientists too as a vital ingredient of most all creative processes.

Longer-term associations or consequences of involvement in the arts.

In the heart of this chapter, replicating the analytical path of Chapter 1, we present comparisons between students extensively and intensively involved in the visual and performing arts during secondary school, and students largely not involved in art, music, drama, or dance during their school years. In this case, the outcomes we assess are attainments and behaviors reported at age 20 and age 26. As readers will see, we conceptualize these outcomes mainly as issues of *Doing Well,* or being successful in societally-rewarded achievements, and *Doing Good,* or engaging in efforts to improve communities and the lives of others.

Long-term profiles: arts-involved versus non-arts-involved students.

How we proceeded. A first step in achieving these comparisons was developing a student-level index of involvement in the arts from data available in the NELS database. We had done the same thing for the analysis in Chapter 1. Now we needed to replicate the arts scale using data from the remaining 12,000 students.

The indicators we used to scale involvement in the arts were the following NELS variables shown in Figure 2.1.

Figure 2.1   NELS variables used to scale student arts involvement

Grade	NELS Variable Name	NELS Variable Label
Grade 8	BYP61BA	R ATTENDS CONCERTS/OTHER MUSICAL EVENTS
	BYP61CA	R GOES TO ART MUSEUMS
	BYP61CB	8TH GRADER GOES TO ART MUSEUMS
	BYS67BF	ATTEND ART AT LEAST ONCE A WEEK
	BYS67BG	ATTEND MUSIC AT LEAST ONCE A WEEK
	BYS67DA	ATTEND DRAMA/SPEECH AT LEAST ONCE A WEEK
	BYS82E	PARTICIPATED IN BAND OR ORCHESTRA
	BYS82F	PARTICIPATED IN CHORUS OR CHOIR
	BYS82G	PARTICIPATED IN DANCE
Grade 10	BYS82N	PARTICIPATED IN DRAMA CLUB
	F1S24H	HOW MUCH COURSEWORK IN ART
	F1S24I	HOW MUCH COURSEWORK IN MUSIC
	F1S24J	HOW MUCH COURSEWORK IN DRAMA
	F1S41BA	PARTICIPATED IN SCHOOL BAND, ORCHESTRA
	F1S41BB	PARTICIPATED IN SCHOOL PLAY OR MUSICAL
	F1S44M	HOW OFTN R TAKES MUSIC, ART, DANCE CLASS
Grade 12	F22XMPP4	MATH LEVEL 4: PROBABILITY OF PROF.
	F2S30BA	PARTICIPATED IN SCHOOL MUSIC GROUP
	F2S30BB	PARTICIPATED IN SCHOOL PLAY OR MUSICAL
	F2S33J	HOW OFTEN R TAKES MUSIC, ART DANCE CLASS

Distribution: Music (12), Theatre (5), Visual Art (4), Dance (3)

The distribution of disciplines that the indicators address is shown at the bottom of Figure 2.1 The indicators correspond roughly to the proportions of the 25,000 students in the original NELS database participating in each arts discipline. Music is the most frequented art discipline in middle and high schools, followed by dance, visual art, and theatre. Disparities in participation vary by grade level and gender.

These indicators were provided mainly by student responses to written surveys. Data recorded in NELS for these indicators were scaled in various ways. One common format was a three choice response: using band as an example, the student *participated, did not participate, or participated as an officer.* This scale led us to assign weights of 0 for non-participation, 1 for participating, and 3 for participating as an officer. (Note: our reasoning for the weight of 3 for officers was that officers are probably the most committed and intensively involved in a discipline, and for the purposes of scaling intensity of involvement, being an officer was a significant signal.)

Another NELS response format scaled the amount of involvement, such as 0 for no courses taken, 1 for a single semester course, 2 for a full school year, 3 for three semesters, and 4 for two full school years. We assigned corresponding numbers to responses in this format as contributors to our scale. A similar format was used for frequency of participation, for example, lessons outside of school, representing less than once per week (1), once per week (2), once or twice per week (3), almost every day (4), and so on.

Having created a scaling system for arts involvement, we turned immediately to the population of greatest interest in this research, namely low-income children. We stress the reasons for this focus above – more advantaged youth are more likely to be involved in art AND to do better in school over time. As described for our early NELS work in Chapter 1, an exclusive focus on youth from low-income families helps level the playing field when it comes to assessing the importance and workings of the arts in a child's life.

We identified the lowest socioeconomic status (SES) quartile within the 12,144 students in our full NELS database. This represented about 3000 students whose parents typically had graduated from high school but had engaged in no further education or formal training, or who had dropped out of school.

Our scale of individual arts involvement ranged from 0 to 40 points. This implies that a few (but very few in actuality) NELS participants reported being completely detached from the arts during secondary school; a music class here and an arts class there are required by many secondary schools. Using this arts involvement scale, we identified the 10 percent of students in the low-SES quartile with the highest arts-involvement scale scores, and the 10 percent of students with the lowest scale scores for involvement in the arts. The two resulting arts-involvement cut-off scores fell this way: the high-arts group scored 16 or higher on our 40 point scale; the low-arts groups scored 4 or fewer points on our scale.

Keeping family background effects out of the analysis. We probed these over-16 and under-4 point groups for an important characteristic – the SES levels of their respective members' families. An important requirement of this study was that the student groups compared on arts engagement levels be as similar as possible on other characteristics that might influence future achievement and development. Critical among the possibilities was that despite hailing from the low-income quartile, SES differences might remain between our two groups, differences that could confuse interpreting differences in outcomes in later survey panels. The average SES scores for our two groups were nearly equal, with a small advantage (about one-tenth of a standard deviation) held by the high-arts group. We decided to remove 12 of the very lowest low-art, low-SES students from our low-arts group. This boosted the average SES level for this group fractionally. We also removed the 5 highest SES scoring students from our high-art, low-SES group. This fractionally lowered the baseline SES average for the high-arts group. We ended up with a high-arts group numbering 341 students, a low-arts group numbering 316 students, and identical average SES scores (to three decimal places) for the two groups.

The group outcome differences we present below are generally expressed as percentages of each group attaining a certain outcome such as finishing college, or comparative percentages of each group participating in a specific activity such as volunteering with youth groups. We organize the displays in a way corresponding to the title of this book, *Doing Well and Doing Good by Doing Art*. We focus on indicators of *doing well* as a young adult. Our *doing well* indicators focused on educational attainments of various descriptions. And we assess *doing good* as a citizen, indicated by participation in various community service activities and volunteering for organizations such as hospitals or youth associations. We also identify voting in public elections as a social contribution.

In reporting, we attend to student outcomes chronologically, that is showing indications of *doing well* and *doing good* recorded at the age of 20, and then parallel indications generated at the age of 26 –12 years after our subjects' first involvement with NELS surveys, tests, and interviews in the 8th grade.

Before we start, what about the arts and high-SES students? While not the central focus of this research, we seized opportunities while performing our data analyses to produce many parallel comparisons for the high-SES quartile of students – that is to compare economically advantaged, highly arts-involved students with economically advantaged students who showed very little engagement in the arts on our involvement scale. We report high-SES comparisons as well as statistics for all NELS students as we proceed. These data can place the low-income arts analyses into useful relief.

The first observation generated by the decision to juxtapose high-SES comparisons was the extreme difference in arts participation shown for students of rich versus poor families that we noted earlier. By design, our high and low-arts groups were about the same size when we considered low-income students, since they respectively represented the highest and lowest 10 percent on our arts-involvement scale. Using the same arts involvement scale-score criteria for sorting the high-income group, the high-SES quartile produced 734 high-arts students (about 25 percent of the entire high-SES group) and only 147 low-arts students (about 5 percent of high-SES students). This works out to a five-fold advantage for students from high-income families.

> *A first observation is the extreme difference in arts participation between students of rich and poor families. Students of high-income families are five times more likely to be highly engaged in the arts in secondary school.*

What do we mean by *doing well* and *doing good*? How do we measure these?

As we have suggested, the NELS database affords multiple perspectives on the activities and accomplishments of its subjects at different age levels. That is the good news. The not so good news is that for any given research project enlisting the database, not every question one would want to have asked was built into the survey. Nor were questions always asked in the ways one might prefer, nor were response choices articulated or arrayed to best get at what one might have in mind. For example, no information about the quality of friendships of NELS participants at age 26 is available; nor are appraisals of qualities or satisfactions with family life. And as for asking questions in our preferred ways, we would have separated questions about taking lessons in music and dance rather than using a question that combines disciplines and where the disciplinary focus of the lesson cannot be discerned.

Research on positive development. Let's consider *doing well* more broadly. There is an extensive literature on what is called positive development focused on adolescents and adolescent transitions to adulthood. One source of insight is the recently published *Encyclopedia of Applied Developmental Science, V.2* (Fisher & Lerner, 2005) that numbers nearly 1000 pages and retails for $600.00. Despite the depth and parsing that so hefty a volume brings to a subject, a very central pair of themes stand out as relevant for our purposes.

Seeming to confound our purpose, there is no precise agreed-upon conception of positive development for adolescents or for effective transitions from adolescents to adulthood. One reason for disagreement is that we embrace ranging meanings of a good life, as individuals and across cultures. Thank goodness. Even in the arts, the dream of a quintessential education in music for one person might be securing virtuoso skills on the violin, for another, an encyclopedic knowledge of the history of jazz, and for another, the gifts of a great composer. In economic life, one person's prize may be earning vast riches, and another's laboring to provide housing in a downtrodden urban center.

If we turn to life satisfaction or happiness, things get very complex. To begin, how satisfied or happy we are flows not according to absolute circumstances, but in significant ways from our individual expectations. When it comes down to it, there is no reason to expect that a ship's steward, a celebrated attorney, a welfare case-worker, a rock-star, or a market cashier will vary systematically or predictably in their life satisfaction levels or happiness. Briefly on our point, if satisfaction or happiness are elements of "doing well," and really they should be, we would be hard-pressed to identify a robust set of predictors of these conditions at the high school age.

But helping us along, definitions of positive development generally point to strengths and virtues in children and adults on the one hand, and buffers or protections from deficit and dysfunction on the other hand (Lerner, Fisher, and Weinberg, 2000). These authors suggest more specifically that we consider five areas when we think of positive human development: competence, confidence, connections, character, and caring. Possible indicators for these attributes abound, some available in NELS and others not. Competence--technical or problem solving skills or the ability to achieve what you want to achieve. Confidence--self-assurance, beliefs that things will go well. Connections--relations with other people and institutions that allow the pursuit of interests and passions and which provide avenues for civic participation. Character--moral values accompanied by moral behavior. Caring--empathy, concern for the welfare of others and society.

If we were to know valid things about an individual in these five domains, we might feel satisfied that we possessed a useful and meaningful set of measures related to "doing well." If we observed variation in our 26-year-olds on these measures--and we surely would--as researchers we might become interested in finding antecedents for *doing well* on each or the collective of measures. As psychologists, we would look in the realms of cognitive and affective development in the early years; we would also locate these developments in the context of family situations. As educators, we would look at variations in the formal learning situations subjects experienced, at participation in focused and meaningful interventions targeting one or more of these positive outcomes. As policy scholars, we would ask which, if any, among factors thought to influence positive outcomes are themselves malleable. In other words, we would look for where we could improve outcomes for individuals and what we could do as a society to improve these outcomes.

Defining positive outcome measures in the NELS database. The designers of the NELS survey did not divide the world of 26-year-olds in a way precisely reflecting the last paragraphs. But we are able to map information from the 4th (age 20) and 5th (age 26) survey panels onto some of the essential ideas represented. Success in advancing education is related to *competence* first. Persisting into the upper reaches of higher education may also be related to *character*, given that honesty and dependability are rewarded in postsecondary education environments and opposing characteristics may curtail careers. Participating in the arts or sports as young adults, reading newspapers, perhaps reading books, and in some sense watching television may be indicators of *connections* with others and society – with the reservation that wholesale preoccupation with any one of these or other activities could limit one's connections to others and institutions. NELS' many indications of voluntarism and community service seem like signs of *caring* for others and society.

Confidence is one positive outcome that seems buried or subsumed in other qualities we can discern from NELS data. During the school years, students responded to questions that support *self-concept* and *locus-of-control* (internal versus external attributions for success) scales. No such scales indicating sense of personal agency or personal confidence about anything specific, or general sense of self-confidence, appear in the NELS out-year data panels. So we did not belabor measures of confidence in our assessments of *doing well* and *doing good*.

Outcome measures for this study. We developed a candidate item pool of 326 indicators for pursuing our quest, including the arts participation and student background information of possible interest.

Figure 2.1b, below, displays the variables from the third and fourth NELS follow-up surveys and interviews that we used to assess outcomes for our students. This is a subset of the variables listed in Appendix A. These variables address the progress of students into and through postsecondary education experiences – more than 80 percent of all NELS high school graduates engaged in some sort of education in subsequent years. These experiences spanned a wide range – from cosmetology and trade schools to M.D. and Ph.D. programs. Some students left high school for the workplace and never looked back. Some entered colleges years after receiving their diplomas. The candidate variables also indicate participation in the labor market, as well as satisfaction with work and education experiences. And a variety of indications of the ways subjects spend their time are available – reading, television watching, participating in sports or the arts, participating in political processes, involvement in religion, and volunteering to assist community organizations and other interest groups.

In the analyses we present shortly, our main focus is on the long-term outcomes for the NELS subjects. That is, what's going on in their lives at age 26. But in presenting our observations, we include indications of various attainments and activities at age 20 – during the spring of the college sophomore year for some, or during the second year of a first job for others, or when about to give birth to a second child for a few, and for most conceivable statuses in between.

Figure 2.1.b   NELS variables used to scale student outcomes at ages 20 and 26

Variable Name	Variable Label
VARATH	Varsity intercollegiate athletics
OTHERATH	Other intercollegiate athletics
PERFARTS	Do performing arts
EDEXPECT	Highest level of education expected
LABR0894	August, 1994 labor status
PRIMSTD3	Primarily student-3 (Jan 1994-interview)
FRMLTRAN	Formal education/training
ACTSTA1	Working full- or part-time
TVWATCH	Numbers hours watch TV weekdays
PARSPORT	Time participating in sports
READING	Time spent reading for pleasure
STRGFRND	Importance of strong friendship
PAYFRNGE	Satisfied with job^s pay/fringe benefits
IMPRTCHA	Satisfied w/job^s importance/challenge
WRKCNDT	Satisfied w/job^s working conditions
OPROMOT	Satisfied w/opport for promotion/advance
VOLUNTE1	Youth organizations-Little League,Scouts
VOLUNTE3	Political clubs or organizations
VOLUNTE4	Church/related (not worship)
VOLUNTE5	Organized volunteer work-hospital work
VOLUNTE6	Sports teams or sports clubs
VOLUNTE7	Educational organizations
VOLUNTE8	Other volunteer work
VOLUNTE9	Volunteer work - none
HRSVLNTR	Hours/week respondent did volunteer work
REGVOTE	Registered to vote
NATELEC	Past 12 months vote local/state
VOTEPRES	Vote in 1992 president election
ENRL0894	PSE: Enrollment status 0894
F3PSEATN	PSE: Highest PSE level attained
F3VOLUNT	Volunteer: Volunteer organization types
F3RGVOTE	Vote: Registered to vote
F3VOTED	Vote: Voted in past elections
F4AACTF	Current activity-full-time job
F4AACTG	Current activity-academic school
F4A12KF	January 2000 activity-full-time job
F4A12KG	January 2000 activity-academic school
F4BSPAY	Job satisfaction-pay
F4BSFRG	Job satisfaction-fringe benefits
F4BSIMP	Job satisfaction-work importance
F4BSPRO	Job satisfaction-promotion opportunity
F4BSED1	Job satisfaction-use of past training
F4BJAUT	Perceived job autonomy

(cont'd)

Figure 2.1.b NELS variables used to scale student outcomes at ages 20 and 26 (cont'd)

Variable Name	Variable Label
F4EFSECT	Sector for first PSE attended
F4ELSECT	Sector for most recent PSE attended
F4EDGR2	Degree/certificate earned-2
F4EGRD	Grades at highest undergrad institution
F4EJOBS	PSE impact-better jobs
F4EHSAL	PSE impact-higher salary
F4ERESP	PSE impact-more responsibility
F4EPROM	PSE impact-promotion opportunity
F4EASP	Educational aspirations by age 30
F4E30CD	Major degree by age 30-code
F4HAIDR	Public aid in 1999
F4HFDST	Public assistance-food stamps
F4HTANF	Public assistance-TANF or AFDC
F4IMAGS	Integration-read papers or magazines
F4IBOOKS	Integration-read books
F4ILIBRY	Integration-go to public library
F4ICULT	Integration-attend plays, concerts
F4IRELIG	Integration-organized religion
F4ISPORT	Integration-participated in sports
F4IYOUTH	Integration-youth organization volunteer
F4ICIVIC	Integration-civic/community volunteer
F4IPOLYL	Integration-political campaign
F4IRVOTE	Registered to vote
F4IVPRE	Voted in 1996 presidential election
F4IVANY	Voted in any election in last 24 months
F4STATUS	Work or postsecondary education status
F4TYPEDG	Types of PSE degrees attained as of 2000
F4ATT4YR	Ever attended a 4-year institution
F4ATTPSE	Ever attended a PSE after HS
F4ENRL00	Currently enrolled in a PSE institution

Indicators of *Doing Well* at age 20. Our indications of *doing well* at age 20 were limited by NELS' offerings. The main indications we included were:

- Being primarily a student during the spring of the second year past high school.
- The type of college the student first attended: particularly a four-year versus two-year college.

We also tracked some specific activities of students that were indications of general social integration or connection: is the student involved in performing arts, in individual or team sports, or in religious activities? How much television is the subject watching at this age? None of these ideas amount to global indicators of well-being, but they do advance portraits of who these 20-year-olds were and what they were up to.

Indicators of *Doing Good* at Age 20. As for *doing good* at age 20, the most fertile offering in the NELS database was the extensive information describing specific volunteer activities. Young adults can be extraordinarily preoccupied with getting the education and training they need to advance on their goals and ambitions, as well as working to support themselves and their families and to meet the costs of education. This may not be a time of extensive giving back to their communities. But more than one-third of all NELS 20-year-olds report engagement in one sort of community service or another at this age. We also include a measure of individual attitudes toward having strong friendships as an indicator of *doing good* at this age.

Indicators of *Doing Well* at Age 26. By age 26, most individuals have completed formal education and most are typically in the labor force. Their educational attainments range widely by this time. We use information about how far subjects progressed through formal education, in what types of institutions, and what degrees they earned along the way as indicators of *doing well*. We also enlist full-time job status and continuing education status in this set of indicators. We include indicators of dependence on public assistance as another suggestion of *doing well*, or not so well, at age 26.

We also set *Doing What* indicators alongside our *Doing Well* assessment. As with the age 20 indicators, these are activities that reflect general social integration and participation. One needn't do any one of these activities, or all of these for that matter, to be considered *doing well*. Non-involvement in most or all of the listed activities might raise concerns about the quality one's life, but we're not here to judge this. These activities include reading books, going to the library, attending plays and concerts, participating in organized religion, and participating in sports.

Indicators of *Doing Good* at Age 26. Our inventory of *Doing Good* indicators at age 26 parallels the indicators we used at age 20. We show indications of volunteering for youth, community, and civic organizations; we also show participation in political campaigns. And we lean on voting bahavior as *doing good* at this age: registering to vote, voting in recent general elections, and voting in the most recent presidential election.

On the nature and quality of NELS survey data.

Readers not familiar with social science or demographic surveys may have questions about the quality of the data obtained when asking subjects to describe themselves and report on their activities. Two types of error can be anticipated in these surveys. One is the random error introduced when individual subjects interpret questions differently, or give more or less care to their question responses, or sometimes mark the wrong bubbles on their response sheets. These sorts of errors would be expected to average themselves out within groups, and also be expected to impact two comparison groups in about the same ways and magnitudes. In addition, it's safe to assume that there may be a small upward bias in self-reports of things that reflect positively on respondents; and a small downward bias where indicators may reflect negatively. This type of error in capturing true scores for individuals does impact group averages on the scales affected. But in practice, the tendency of respondents to exaggerate or minimize in survey self-reports has shown to be small. Even self-reports of academic grades have a good reputation in education research.[xxv] We don't have reasons at the outset to believe that our groups would differ in their tendencies to exaggerate or minimize when responding to specific questions in the NELS survey. Thus the absolute levels reported, say of service to youth groups, may overstate their true values modestly, but they will do so similarly for both groups under scrutiny.[xxvi] And group differences would show reasonably accurately.

Results – Comparing Low-income Students *High* in Arts Involvement and Low-income Students *Low* in Arts Involvement

***Doing well* and *doing what* at Age 20.** Figure 2.2 displays indications of the status and activities of our select groups of NELS subjects as of the third follow-up panel. Included are indications of education status and a limited number of activities reported on through the survey. In all comparisons between arts-involved and not arts-involved groups, statistically significant advantages for one or the other group are indicated in **bold** text.

We direct a main focus within the table to the two right-most columns. Here we show data for the two primary groups of interest in this chapter, and in this book for the most part. These are the low-income, or low-SES, students who registered as the most highly involved in the visual and performing arts (Hi Art) on the one hand, and the least involved in the arts (Low Art) on the other hand. The groups numbered 341 and 316 subjects respectively. As described above, these two groups represent about the highest ten percent and lowest ten percent of all low-SES subjects in terms of engagement in the arts. As a reminder, our entire pool of NELS subjects included the 12,144 students who participated in all five data collection panels between the ages of 14 and 26.

Education. About 80 percent of high-arts students and 75 percent of low-arts students reported being a student at age 20. Twenty-nine percent of high-arts students first enrolled in four-year colleges. Only 11.4 percent of low-arts students did so. Roughly 30 percent in both groups enrolled first in two-year colleges.

On the *doing what* side of the ledger, nine percent of the arts group reported doing performing arts – outpacing the low-arts group by a factor of 30 to 1 on this measure. Nearly half of the arts students also reported participating in religious activities at age 20, the corresponding figure for the low-arts groups was just over one-third. No significant differences between the groups show in sports participation or television watching, but the measures in these two areas are slightly higher for the low-arts group.

Figure 2.2

Indicators of early postsecondary education and other activities at age 20, by SES and arts involvement groups. Percentages by group.

		All Students	Hi SES Students		Low SES Students	
Doing Well			**_Hi Art_**	**_Low Art_**	**_Hi Art_**	**_Low Art_**
Primarily a student in Jan 1994		85.1	94.2	93.2	80.8	74.8
Sector for first college attended	2-year	29.3	12	**24.5**	30.5	27.2
	4-year	42.3	**83.8**	61.9	**29.0**	11.4
Doing What?						
Does performing arts		2.3	**9.7**	0.6	**9.0**	0.3
Participates in sports		49.0	51	52.4	39	45.9
Participates in religious activities		39.6	**48.5**	38.8	**48.7**	34.2
3 or more hours of TV on weekdays		34.5	20.8	27.3	43.1	45.8

Bold figures indicate between-group percentage differences significant at p < .05 or better (Chi square, df2 >3.84).

> *When compared to students lacking arts participation, the highly arts-involved are more likely to still be a student at age 20 (about 81 versus 75 percent within the respective groups), and more than twice as likely to have initially enrolled in a 4-year college.*

High-SES group comparisons. Figure 2.2 shows the same comparisons for the highest SES quartile, displaying contrasts between the highest and lowest arts participants among these high-income students. In this quartile, students' parents typically completed a college bachelor's degree or graduate level studies and degrees. The contrasts are similar to those we found for low-SES students. Within the high-SES group, the high-arts students are more likely to start out in four-year colleges, are ten times more likely to continue activities in the performing arts beyond high school, and more likely to be involved in religious activities. The low-arts student in the high-SES group is twice as likely to enroll in a two-year college as the high-art student. Both low and high-arts students in the high-SES group were very likely to have been students at age 20 (93 and 94 percent respectively).

Two implications stand out. We see the continuation of advantages reported at grade 12 for high-arts students; also the stark contrasts between high-SES and low-SES students. One implication is that comparative advantages with which the low-income high-arts students finished high school appear to lead to an extended leg-up on their subsequent achievements. While enrollment in a two-year college can be the first step in an educational course leading to a bachelor's degree or further academic or professional studies, enrolling in a four-year college boosts the probability of higher educational accomplishments. The second implication of the data shown in Figure 2.2 flows from some global comparisons between the high-SES and low-SES students, ignoring arts engagement differences. High-SES students are far more likely to be a student at age 20, far more likely to enroll in a four-year college, considerably less likely to enroll in a two-year college, and less likely to watch 3 or more hours of television per weekday.

All-student comparisons. We include in most of our presentations data that describe the averages on all measures for the entire 12,144 students in the database. These are included as a point of reference for the specific group data reported. Occasionally, comparisons between our select groups and the entire population lend meaning to the data and place the importance of the arts in some relief. For example, in Figure 2.2 we report that 9 percent of high-arts, low-income kids indicate doing performing arts as of age 20. In comparison, only 2.3 percent of *all* students report doing performing arts at this point in their lives. Another example shows in Figure 2.3. We report here that 27.9 percent of all 12,000+ students report doing any volunteer work at age 20, while more than 37 percent of low-income, high-arts students report doing some form of volunteer work.

> *Observed patterns have a general form. Low-SES students fall short of the average student in the whole sample on most achievement and attainment measures. But in some instances, the low-income, high-arts student outperforms not only her low-arts counterpart, but also outperforms the average student in the entire database.*

Doing Good **at Age 20.** Our indicators of *doing good* at this age concentrate on volunteer service. The NELS third follow-up, at age 20, contained at least eight indicators of service to various types of organizations. Indicators for our five groups are shown in Figure 2.3.

Figure 2.3

Indicators of community service activities at age 20, by SES and arts involvement groups. Percentages by group.

Doing Good	All Students	Hi SES Students		Low SES Students	
		Hi Art	*Low Art*	*Hi Art*	*Low Art*
Volunteer work - any	27.9	**61**	45.6	**37.2**	19.6
Volunteered at hospitals	10.6	**24.1**	13.6	**7.9**	4.1
Volunteered, youth orgs, scouts	9.4	**15.5**	11.6	**7.9**	3.2
Vol. sports teams or sports clubs	6.4	9.9	10.2	4.1	2.5
Vol. church/related (not worship)	11.4	**18.8**	8.8	**16.7**	7.3
Vol. educational organizations	6.2	**16.5**	7.5	**5.9**	1.4
Vol. political clubs or organizations	3.1	**8.2**	3.4	**2.7**	1.0
Other volunteer work	7.1	**12.5**	10.2	**7.6**	3.5
Registered to Vote	70.2	**80.8**	72.8	**70.7**	50.9
Strong friendships very important	86.0	**93.6**	85	**82.4**	75.3

Bold figures indicate between-group percentage differences significant at p < .05 or better (Chi square, df2 >3.84).

Low-income students: high-arts vs. low-arts. Following what will become a familiar format, Figure 2.3 shows comparisons suggesting differences the arts make when it comes to voluntarism, voting, and friendships. As with other displays, the numbers indicate within group percentages. For example in the top right, 37.2 percent of the high-arts, low-SES students reported doing some type of volunteer work as of age 20. The corresponding percentage for the low-arts, low-SES group was 19.6 percent. This is a sizeable difference.

The meaning of statistical significance in these displays:

Statistically significant differences noted by bold figures in our tables are differences that are unlikely to have occurred by chance or random measurement error. In all of our tables, we use a 95 percent confidence standard. This means that for the differences we show as significant, the chances that the displayed difference resulted from random chance is less than five percent. Or turning this around, we're 95 percent confident that the difference between the groups is real.

The careful observer will note that differences in the 8 to 9 percentage point range seem to be required for statistical significance when the percentages in our tables are between about 30 and 70 percent. At the tail ends of the percentage distributions, for example in the Other Volunteer Work *category in Figure 2.3, the difference standard is smaller – here about a 4 percentage point difference is required for statistical significance when one group stands at 7.6 percent.*

Finally, across the different charts ahead, the sample sizes differ depending on which groups we are comparing. Larger sample sizes mean smaller differences may be statistically significant; smaller sample sizes require larger estimated differences for those differences to be considered significant.

The statistical test for significance of percentage differences between groups is the Chi Square test, as noted at the bottom of each table.

How do low- and high-arts groups compare on *doing good* measures at age 20?

Returning to Figure 2.3 above, the high-arts, low-SES group compares favorably on most dimensions of voluntary work at age 20. As mentioned, more than one-third of students in this group report doing some sort of volunteer work, while less than one-fifth within the counterpart low-arts group report volunteering. The percentages volunteering in the individual categories tend to be small – single digits typically. But in five of the seven areas – hospitals, youth groups, church groups, educational organizations, and other volunteer work – the high-arts students prevail. The greatest difference reported for the individual categories shows up in volunteering for church-related organizations. Various indications of high involvement in church related voluntarism by students engaged in the arts show up as we go forward.

The high-arts group reports significantly higher voter registrations at age 20 than its low-arts counterpart and a modestly higher yet significant indication that they consider strong friends to be very important.

Low- versus high-SES groups. Voluntarism among our high-income groups, arts involved or not, is greater than what we found for low-income sample members. The relative advantages shown for high-arts students within the high-income group are comparable to those shown for low-SES students – the arts-involved students report more voluntarism.

Low-income, high-arts students versus the average student. The low-income student intensively involved in the arts over the secondary school years reports more engagement in volunteer work at age 20 than the average student in the whole NELS sample at the same age (37.2 percent versus 27.9 percent). The low-income, high-arts student essentially matches the average student in other areas also – registering to vote, regard for strong friendships, volunteering for political or educational organizations, youth organizations, and hospitals. These data suggest important differences, i.e., advantages for the low-income arts students.

> *The low-income student intensively involved in the arts over the secondary school years reports more engagement in volunteer work at age 20 than the average student in the whole NELS sample at the same age (37.2 percent versus 27.9 percent). And far more than his low-income, low-arts counterpart (37.2 percent versus 19.6 percent).*

Doing Well and *Doing Good* at Age 26 – the Final NELS Panel

Figures 2.4, 2.5, and 2.6 display information from the NELS fourth follow-up survey, organized along the lines of what we showed for the third follow-up. At age 26, the NELS participants have been out of high school for eight years, and for some, out of college for four years. Most students have completed formal education, families are forming or established, most participants are in the labor force, a few continue advanced studies, and a non-trivial share express hopes to finish college degrees by age 30.

The fifth data panel (age 26) contained more information than the fourth (age 20) about post-secondary education experiences. This reflects the fact that much in the way of actions, behaviors, and decisions concerning college-going and postsecondary training occurs after the age of 20, when the prior round of data collection took place. So now we benefit from information about college attendance, grades earned during college, and degrees awarded.

NELS subjects have not only engaged in postsecondary education, they have also had time to appraise how they benefited from the experiences. We include such appraisals, which turn out to show marked differences across our arts and non-arts groups. We also continue to explore integrative sorts of activities for our samples, including reading books, going to public libraries, attending plays and concerts, and participating in religion or sports. Fewer, more consolidated indicators of community service are available and enlisted, as well as repeat measures of voting behavior.

As suggested above, if we were to ask a 26-year-old how she was doing, we would expect answers reflecting a diverse set of life conditions and qualities:

"Well, I graduated from college since I last saw you, I'm now working in a chemistry laboratory and have a pushy supervisor, I'm getting married in June – for the second time, I have my own car, and we're saving for a condominium near work. My parents and sisters are all doing well, and our landlord let us have a dog last year, which has cost us nearly a thousand dollars so far. Other than the dog, we're all healthy."

Figure 2.4

Indicators of higher education and employment-related attainment at age 26,

by SES and arts involvement groups. Percentages by group.

		All Students	_Hi SES Students_		_Low SES Students_	
Doing Well			_Hi Art_	_Low Art_	_Hi Art_	_Low Art_
Ever attended college after high school		79.1	98.6	92.5	**70.7**	48.1
Ever attended 4-yr post-sec. institution		53.8	**93.3**	76.0	**38.7**	16.8
Mostly As and Bs as undergraduate		31.0	36.8	55.0	14.7	8.5
Degree/certificate earned-2000	MA+	3.8	12.1	10.9	**0.8**	0.3
	BA+	29.6	**17.7**	6.3	**17.7**	6.3
	Assoc +	36.9	**26.8**	10.7	**24.0**	10.3
Holding full time job, 2000		75.3	71.3	74.8	75.1	69.3
Attending academic institution, 2000		17.5	28.2	24.5	**11.7**	6.6
Neither work nor academic study, 2000		7.2	0.5	0.7	13.2	**24.1**
Dependence on public assistance						
Public aid in 1999		3.1	0.3	**3.4**	4.1	**8.5**
Public assistance-food stamps		2.3	0.3	**3.4**	2.9	**7.9**

Bold figures indicate between-group percentage differences significant at p < .05 or better (Chi square, df2 >3.84).

Even if the NELS database contained information permitting us to describe respondents in these areas, we wouldn't use the full spread of data for this study. We are mainly interested in the effects that an arts-rich secondary education have on individual lives. We focus primarily on educational effects that may be impacted by differing sorts of early educational experiences. We also focus on connections between education experiences and success in the labor market – securing and keeping rewarding jobs are widely held personal goals. Our *doing well* indicators concentrate in these two realms – education and employment.

As we displayed for age 20 in the previous figure, Figure 2.4 displays comparisons between our arts-involved and non-arts-involved 26-year-olds. The right two columns address our main focus – the long-term fortunes of low-income students. The most dramatic evidence of *doing well*, evidence suggesting that high involvement in the arts during secondary school pays off for low-SES students, shows up as success in college – completing four-year college programs and higher likelihood of earning degrees at all levels by age 26.

> *Dramatic evidence of doing well, indicating that high involvement in the arts during secondary school pays off for poor students, shows up as success in college – higher rates of completing college programs and earning college and postgraduate degrees by age 26.*

By age 26, the following *doing well* comparisons between high-arts and low-arts students from the lowest SES ranks in high school stand out:

Attending college at all. More than 70 percent of the high-arts group attended college after high school. About 50 percent of the low-arts group attended college after high school.

Attending 4-year colleges. Nearly 40 percent of high-arts students enrolled in four-year colleges. Just under 17 percent of low-arts students did so.

***Doing well* in college.** Nearly 15 percent of high-arts students earned mostly A's and B's in their most recent college. Between 8 and 9 percent of low-arts students performed this well.

Degrees earned. Disparities between high-arts and low-arts low-income students stand out starkly. High-arts students were nearly three times as likely to have earned BA degrees (about 18 percent versus 6 percent) more than twice as likely to have earned associate degrees, and nearly three times as likely to have earned masters or higher degrees.

Still enrolled at age 26. While the percentages are fairly small, about 12 percent of high-arts 26-year-olds were still attending college at the NELS fourth follow-up; only 7 percent of the low-arts students were still enrolled. This appears to support a contention that the high-arts students systematically strived more for college attainment.

The differences between high-arts and low-arts students in education success are dramatic by any definition. As we describe in the concluding section of this chapter, it appears that the education-related gaps between high-arts and low-arts students became wider as the NELS surveys proceed to the later panels – paralleling the increasing advantages over grades 8 through 12 in Chapter 1.

The differences between high-arts and low-arts students in education success are dramatic by any definition. The education-related gaps between high-arts and low-arts students became wider as the NELS subjects progressed to age 26.

How well did postsecondary education "work" for NELS students? The NELS survey designers posed an unusual set of questions to the 26 year-olds, questions that probed how their college and postsecondary training experiences may have helped them meet their goals and contributed to successful work experiences.

Figure 2.5 shows these questions and how the high-arts and low-arts groups responded.

Figure 2.5

Indicators of perceived value of post-secondary education experiences to age ; by SES and arts involvement groups. Percentages by group.

Personal Outlook	All Students	Hi SES Students		Low SES Students	
		Hi Art	Low Art	Hi Art	Low Art
Satisfaction with work					
Job satisfaction-pay	69.5	70.2	63.3	69.8	73.7
Job satisfaction-fringe benefits	70.9	71.4	76.2	66.9	63.3
Job satisfaction-work importance	80.3	79.8	76.9	83.3	80.7
Job satisfaction-promotion opportunity	66.3	64.7	67.3	67.2	65.8
Job satisfaction-use of past training	75.8	78.6	77.6	75.7	71.8
Job autonomy (some decisions/own boss)	64.8	66.8	63.9	64.8	59.2

In comparison to low-arts students, high-arts students got further in college spent more time in four-year colleges and acquired more and higher degrees. It may not be surprising then that high-arts students hold more affirmative beliefs

Figure 2.5 displays these measures:

- Leading to better jobs
- Leading to higher pay
- Leading to jobs with more responsibility

- Leading to jobs with more promotion opportunity
- Leading to even further aspirations.

On all but the issue of job pay, about 50 percent more high-arts students than low-arts students agreed that their education experiences through age 26 brought them such benefits. While NELS did not scale the importance of each of these potential developments to participants, it does not stretch the imagination to suggest that "better" jobs, more responsibility, and more opportunities for advancement are critical components of *doing well* as a young adult, and are themselves elements of a life one could call satisfying. In addition, advancing the educational achievements and attainments of young citizens is widely considered an important element of enhancing the global economic, political, and social success of the nation – societal ambitions proving difficult to advance on in recent years. And beliefs that education leads to the dreams and ambitions of individuals might be considered among the elemental dispositions holding a democracy together.

What about *Doing Good* at age 26?

Figure 2.7 shows indications of selected pastimes and activities of 26 year-olds, activities that are suggestive of a young adult life integrated with the community. This figure also shows specific behaviors that would be called *doing good* for the community or society. In general, the high-arts students perform more positively on these measures than the low-arts students. Some of these differences, such as in reading books or going to the library, are probably driven by group differences in the age-26 education levels we have documented. We have and will make arguments that motivations and dispositions that contribute to educational striving may be impacted by early extensive arts education experiences. Attending plays and concerts would seem directly impacted by high-arts versus low-arts status, conditions that should bear on simple interest in the performing arts.

High-arts students are ten to twenty percent more likely to:

- Read books
- Frequent a public library
- Participate in organized religion.
- Attend plays and concerts (borderline statistically significant)

Figure 2.6

Indicators of activities and community service involvement at age 26,

by SES and arts involvement groups. Percentages by group.

Doing What?	All Students	Hi SES Students		Low SES Students	
		Hi Art	Low Art	Hi Art	Low Art
Read papers or magazines 3+ days/wk.	67.8	74.0	74.2	76.5	75.0
Read any books	81	91.7	87.1	**81.8**	73.8
Ever go to public library	48.4	51.3	51.7	**55.1**	43.0
Ever attend plays, concerts	62.4	83.2	76.2	56.4	48.1
Participate in organized religion	56.2	62.8	55.8	**64.8**	47.8
Participate in sports	46.3	43.1	49.0	44.1	41.1
Doing Good					
Youth organization volunteer	20	27.5	19.7	**24.3**	10.8
Civic/community volunteer	21.5	35.1	20.4	**24.6**	10.4
Participate in political campaign	3.6	7.1	1.4	4.1	2.8
Registered to vote	76.4	86.1	83.7	**77.7**	67.1
Voted in any election, past 24 mos.	41.2	53.5	53.7	37	30.4
Voted, 1996 Presidential election (age 22)	55	71.7	61.9	**52.5**	35.1

Bold figures indicate between-group percentage differences significant at p < .05 or better (Chi square, df2 >3.84)

Low-arts students fail to lead high-arts students in any of our *Doing What* category.

In the realm of *doing good*, the high-arts students are more active as community and youth volunteers across various groups, and both register and vote more frequently.

High-arts students are more than twice as likely as low-arts students to:

- Volunteer for a youth organization
- Volunteer for a civic or community organization.

In addition, high-arts students are about 15 percent more likely to register to vote, more than 30 percent more likely to have voted in the most recent presidential election, and about 20 percent more likely to have voted in any election in the 24 months leading to the last NELS survey panel.[xxvii]

> *By age 26, high-arts NELS participants scored significantly higher than low-arts students on measures of socially integrated activities (attending plays and concerts, participating in organized religion, frequenting libraries and reading books). High-arts students also showed more than twice as much community and youth volunteer service and a significant edge in voting registration and voting itself.*

High-SES students? Our *doing good* measures for high-SES high-arts versus low-arts students show patterns analogous to those displayed for low-SES high and low-arts students. A number of advantages stand out for high-arts students, and general levels of positive outcomes are higher than for both low-SES groups.

Conclusions to this point.

This chapter extends the first round of high-school focused analyses we reported in "Involvement in the Arts and Success in Secondary School" in 1999.[xxviii] What evidenced as significant differences between students highly engaged in the arts during their last five years of secondary school are not only sustained into and beyond the college years, the differences become larger. The areas affected are pervasive and include:

- Academic grades
- Standardized test scores in reading, language, mathematics, and history
- Early attitudes about civic involvement

- Actual voluntarism and civic involvement as young adults
- More registering to vote and voting
- Reading more books and newspapers
- More library use
- Increased participation in organized religion

- Doing and attending performing arts

- Two-fold differences in eligibility and attendance at four-year colleges
- Corresponding large differences in earning BA and higher degrees by age 26
- Holding full-time jobs as young adults, and
- Less eventual dependence on public assistance including AFDC and Food Stamps.

A final perspective – high-arts students versus the *average low-income* student.

The practical choices that students and families make are not typically between such things as very high-arts involvement and very low-arts involvement. Decisions are usually made concerning what involvements to take on and at what levels they will be pursued. Our final two analyses try to capture this by drawing comparisons between the low-income, high-arts students and low-income students generally. This removes the influence of possible factors that might accompany being extremely low-arts in the contrasts we drew above. Students extremely lacking involvement in the arts have some chance of being generally disengaged in high school, which would probably work to their detriment.

Figure 2.7

Comparing Low-income High Art and All Low-income Students, Percentages in Each Group, Age 20

		N	2777	341
Doing Well -- Age 20			All Low Income Students	Hi Art, Low-income
Primarily a student in Jan 1994			65.1	**71**
Current activity full time job			**75.3**	69.3
Sector for first college attended	2-year		29.1	30.5
	4-year		18.8	**29.0**
Doing What -- Age 20				
Does performing arts			3.1	**9.0**
Participates in sports			43.5	39
Participates in religious activities			35.4	**48.7**
3 or more hours of TV on weekdays			44.8	43.1
Doing Good -- Age 20			All Low Income Students	Hi Art, Low-income
Volunteer work - any			28.0	**37.2**
Volunteered at hospitals			5.4	_7.9_
Volunteered, youth orgs, scouts			5.5	_7.9_
Vol. sports teams or sports clubs			4.5	4.1
Vol. church/related (not worship)			9.7	**16.7**
Vol. educational organizations			3.4	**5.9**
Vol. political clubs or organizations			1.2	**2.7**
Other volunteer work			5.5	_7.6_
Strong friendships very important			86.0	82.4

Bold figures indicate advantages for students involved in art compared to all students in the NELS:88 low SES quartile. percentage differences significant at p < 0.05 or better (Chi square, df2 >3.84).
Underscored figures are significant at p < 0.10 or better.

Figure 2.7 shows comparisons in *doing well* and *doing good* measures for the average low-income, high-arts student versus the average low-income student. An advantage in enrolling in 4-year colleges stands out, as does the predictable "doing more performing arts" statistic. The arts group is considerably more likely to participate in religious activities (48.7 percent to 35.4 percent) as well as to participate in any sort of volunteer work (37.2 percent to 28.0 percent). A large difference in volunteering behavior is in the church-related area.

As we survey this table and consider previous comparisons for high-arts students, there is a consistent pattern of comparatively high involvement in religious activities and volunteering for religious organizations by high-arts students. We note this here for more detailed exploration – for a follow-up analysis and article perhaps that might track both the gender and religion questions we have identified but do not address in this book.

Figure 2.8 shows the same comparisons for our students at age 26. By this time, additional advantages have emerged for low-income, high-arts students in comparison to the average low-income student. The college attainment measures differ materially. High-arts students were more likely ever have been a postsecondary education student, to ever have attended a four-year college, and to have earned bachelors or associate degrees.

Student reflections on their own education show consistent differences or advantages for the high-arts group here. They report that their postsecondary education has impacted their lives in the workplace substantially up to age 26. High-arts students are more likely to say that their education has led to better jobs, higher pay, increased job responsibility, and more promotion opportunities.

> By many comparisons, low-income, high-arts students show stronger indicators of accomplishment in and value for their educations when compared to the average low-income student. Both groups report similar levels of involvement in community service.

❋ ❋ ❋

(Figure 2.8 on following page.)

Figure 2.8

Comparing Low-income High Art and All Low-income Students, Percentages in Each Group, Age 26

		All Low Income Students	Hi Art, Low-income
	N	12441	341
Doing Well -- Age 26			
Ever attended college after high school		59.3	**70.7**
Ever attended 4-yr post-sec. institution		26.9	**38.7**
Mostly As and Bs as undergraduate		18.7	14.7
Degree/certificate earned-2000	MA+	0.7	0.8
	BA+	10.4	**17.7**
	Assoc +	17.2	**24.0**
Holding full time job, 2000		69.4	**75.1**
Full time study, 2000		**4.8**	2.1
Dependence on public assistance			
Public aid in 1999		2.1	**4.1**
Public assistance-food stamps		**4.6**	2.9
Doing What -- Age 26			
Read papers or magazines 3+ days/wk.		67.8	**76.5**
Read any books		81	**81.8**
Ever go to public library		48.4	**55.1**
Ever attend plays, concerts		62.4	56.4
Participate in organized religion		56.2	**64.8**
Participate in sports		46.3	44.1
Doing Good -- Age 26		**All Low Income Students**	**Hi Art, Low-income**
Youth organization volunteer		20	**24.3**
Civic/community volunteer		21.5	**24.6**
Participate in political campaign		3.6	**4.1**
Registered to vote		76.4	**77.7**
Voted in any election, past 24 mos.		41.2	37
Voted, 1996 Presidential election (age 22)		55	**52.5**
Reflections on Own Education			
Education has led to better jobs		41.2	**50.7**
Education has led to higher pay		37.0	**45.2**
Education has led to more responsibility		42.6	**54.5**
Education leads to promotion opportunity		38.1	**48.1**
aspire to BA+ by age 30		29.7	36.7

Bold figures indicate advantages for students involved in either art or sports compared to students involved in neither, percentage differences significant at p < .05 or better (Chi square, df2 >3.84).

Continued exploration of what propels advantages for the high-arts students.

We remind readers that our student tracking procedures in this study began with cohorts of 8th grade students who were matched precisely in measured family education and income (socioeconomic status) levels. Their divergence in status and performance over time thus cannot be attributed to any family support that would strictly be captured in family SES measures. This is not to say that their families did not systematically differ in ways that could have mattered – more on this as we go forward. The two groups we compare were both from the lowest SES quartile – with a parent or parents who finished high school and went no further in their formal education, or who had dropped out of school without earning a high school diploma. And within this group of about 3,000 low-income students still participating in NELS over its five waves of data collection, we identified about 300 students as very highly involved in the arts, the top 10 percent, and another 300 students who had little or no involvement in school music, visual art, theatre, or dance activities (the bottom 10 percent). So the primary difference between our two groups was their measured participation in the visual and performing arts.

Why these differences emerged and grew over time is surely a more complicated question. A mix of factors was probably at play. We'll introduce these now, and have more to say about each as subsequent chapters unfold. Plausible reasons for the advantages shown for arts-engaged poor students include:

Cognitive effects of learning and doing arts. Many research studies have shown impacts of arts learning and participation on cognition – the way children think and solve problems, and in a limited number of studies, the way their brains process experiences and information. In its most general form, any experience or activity is reflected in neural activity, and any experience or activity repeated over time has the tendency to reinforce or develop specific neural pathways – albeit 10,000 replications will not necessarily perfect a golf swing. But sustained pursuit of most anything tends to "rewire" the brain. In this study, the high-arts students are engaged in repeated arts-related experiences – sustained music lessons, drawing and painting over a period of years, playing ever more complex roles on stage, or dancing and choreographing as a principle young-life passion. These brains underwent some changes over the high school years. If the rewiring leaves such engaged students better able to accomplish things beyond the arts – that is if there is a general transfer of cognitive capacity to non-arts domains – some of the advantages we show for arts-involved students may have come from increased brainpower. The music and spatial reasoning studies are a good example of this, as is the recent work of Schellenberg (2004) and Catterall and Rauscher (2008).[xxix] We explore the neurology of cognitive transfer in more detail in Chapter 5.

Enhancing motivation. A number of studies have shown that gaining mastery in the arts leads children to feel a sense of accomplishment, and that such self-beliefs may spill over into non-arts areas of life. Studies of learning in the visual arts have shown parallel developments between artistic accomplishment and individual sense of personal agency or self-efficacy. If our high-arts students gained personal agency and efficacy through their five years of intensive arts experiences, their self-beliefs may have contributed to their evident alignments with dominant educational and social values. They were more determined to get ahead and saw education as a path to this outcome. Moreover, they believed that they could succeed. That's a rather good translation of self-efficacy.

The contributions of artistic cultures. It may be that artistic cultures present in schools or artistic communities help students develop particular values, orientations, and dispositions that promote success. Recent studies of "arts-rich schools" suggest this very thing. The arts have been characterized to reflect diverse ways of knowing as well as creativity and diverse ways of showing what you know and are able to do. Cultures develop around musically- or theatrically-involved groups of students that may support collaboration, cooperation, and the sense that community contribution and support matter. Recent works of The Arts Education Partnership, Horowitz & Webb-Dempsey, and Noblit suggest that there is something different and positive about arts rich schools.[xxx] As it turns out, the NELS database is uniquely positioned to provide rigorous information on the potential influences of arts-rich schools. We devote Chapters 4 and 5 to this subject.

Early developments probably lead to expanding prospects.
In *Champions of Change*[xxxi] we reported that by 12th grade, high-arts students were better off on a number of counts, academically and socially. We argued that involvement in the arts contributed to these advantages. It's reasonable to think that leaving high school with the comparatively advantaged academic and social profiles we found would lead to advantages in getting along in later life – succeeding in college and the workplace, carrying forward community and social inclinations. This is a sticky prospect as an explanation, even though it undoubtedly bears some truth. If the arts produced the differences that mattered which showed at age 18, the arts may claim some responsibility for what happens to students beyond high school as a simple matter of preparation and orientation.

At the same time, it has been argued that the arts impact the way we think as well as our important values. If such characteristics emerge in secondary school, they probably persist long beyond the school years. What then matters is the important effects of such artistic foundations on how we go about our lives later on – the effectiveness of our thinking and what motivates us to behave and interact the way we do.

Involvement in the arts breeds future involvement in the arts. We'll go out on a limb here. If there is one association between school-based engagement in the arts and behavior as young adults that the causation-focused theorist would not challenge, it is that our high-arts students engage in performing arts activities and attend artistic performances more regularly as young adults. We don't need exotic theory to explain this. We could go on to examine the roles of active arts participation and attendance in the lives of young adults, a prospect that in fact could be explored with NELS age 26 data. But that's for another day.

The value of passionate engagement in high school.

Research has suggested that earnest engagement and involvement during school leads to success. Studies of school dropouts in the early panels of the NELS data suggest that student involvement in a variety of areas tends to reduce dropout rates.[xxxii] Panels of school dropouts frequenting the work of this author in the late 1980s and early 1990s produced comments along the lines of, "Well, when it was basketball season, I always came to school. When it wasn't, I didn't. Finally, I just quit." If only basketball season had been nine months long!

Studies in higher education are especially emphatic about the importance of engagement and involvement on college campuses. The works of Robert Pace and Alexander Astin[xxxiii] and colleagues show unambiguously that involvement is a strong predictor of finishing college, a domain where attrition rates remain significant.

Our early work reported in Chapter 1 generated a number of questions about the importance of engagement, the main challenge being that perhaps the main factor producing our observed advantages was largely the *engagement of students at this crucial time in their lives*. A great many times over recent years, a sort of question was posed to us that can be summed up as, "Is it the arts? Are sports any different?"

Without attempting yet to do more sorting among possible explanations for our findings, we now turn directly to this very question in Chapter 3. *Are sports any different?*

James S. Catterall

Chapter 3: Is it the Arts?
Would high school sports have the same effects?

Is intensive engagement during high school per se the main issue?

In this chapter, we offer an analysis of intensive involvement in sports in high school – following the methods used to track involvement in the arts in Chapter 2. One motivation for pursuing this work was the many questions tossed at us after our NELS high school arts study was published. This was the question: is it the arts that produce these effects, or could it be high engagement in a school activity shown by these kids more generally? One version of this question: is basketball any different

Research context of this investigation. The arts experiences we assessed in Chapter 2 can fall into the larger class of adolescent activities considered to be in part, or mostly, extracurricular. The arts are sometimes more integrated into the school curriculum than other extracurricular activities – courses in visual arts or music may be scheduled into the academic day and fulfill graduation requirements, the English department may hold formal classes in theatre. Dance may have it's own school department but may be housed in physical education, where dance classes leading to grades on transcripts also take place. Each of the arts may be offered in out-of-school time – after-school rehearsals, weekend day and evening performances, weekend art displays, evening master classes.

In general, studies of extracurricular activities have concentrated on activities many of us would readily list if asked to provide an inventory – athletics and music head the list – the basketball or football teams, the school orchestra, the marching band. A long list of clubs follows ranging from theatre and debate societies to dance associations and the chess club.

Research on extracurricular activities, like much research on child-development and educational achievement, is populated by studies rife with limiting features common to social science and psychological research. The most problematic is that few studies are longitudinal and thus most are ill equipped to discern patterns of influence or causation (Hartmann, 2008). We do find some studies following students for a year and some times two or three years (e.g. Darling, 2004). But these are typically insufficient periods of time in which to capture enduring academic or social effects. Beyond this limitation, available studies do not tend to focus on the *effects* of engagement in extracurricular activities. Popular studies examine gender and racial differences in who chooses which activities. Others probe why students choose the particular activities they do, and perhaps group (family background / ethnic) differences in these choices.

One reason for attention to descriptions of participation in extracurricular activities is quite reasonable – as already noted, the authors realize that short periods of engagement are not expected to produce effects that stand up to tests of material or statistical significance. Another explanation is reasonable too: a consensus exists among adolescent development researchers that beyond individual differences in cognitive and emotional capacity, and beyond differences in the family circumstances enveloping and nurturing growing children and adolescents, extra-curricular activities may turn out to have little effect on the core outcomes researchers pose or hope to find. And this points to an accepted global assessment in this literature we touched on briefly in Chapter 2 – this is that thus far the reported effects of extracurricular activities on positive adolescent development are small.[xxxiv] This is not to say that small scale, idiosyncratic studies of the basketball players in Cuyahoga County would not find substantially higher graduating rates for participants, or that legions of small non-generalizable studies couldn't point clearly to the importance of various past-times and school-based organizations that occupy our youth.

Presence versus Quality of an activity. A dimension of engagement vitally important to the NELS study, whether the subject in question is art, or athletics, or any other specific activities, relates to the quality and intensity of the experience in question. Some studies conceptualize participation as a yes or no proposition – "Please check the boxes to indicate what you did in the past year." Some studies ask how many hours per day or week the student spends playing baseball, or in rehearsal and production for the school musical. These measure take a step in the direction of extent or intensity of engagement. Some students on the baseball team meander and pick crabgrass in right field most of each afternoon. Others toss a hundred balls from third to first base and practice situation strategy with their teammates on a daily basis. Some in the theatre society consider their efforts at lighting a production to be the most important element of the enterprise and put in overtime hours to get this right – and experience pride and accomplishment in their work. Others in the theatre club persist, but languish in the smallest of parts or jobs and devote their attention elsewhere for the most part.

If baseball or theatre participation were to have effects on participating students, we'd expect the effects to be vastly different in the contrasting types of participation just described. A main point here is that the way social science and education research are usually carried out, and the way many of the indicators developed surveys such as NELS in fact materials, simple individual indications, like a bubbled-in number if you play an individual sport, do nothing to characterize the experience. But our "intense involvement" criteria help out on this issue.

Earlier, we described our use of multiple indicators of arts involvement in Chapter 2. We also pointed out that by identifying students whose in-school and out of school lives looked to be highly infused with arts-related activities, we could assemble a sample that could inform us about such arts-rich lives. These were no mere members of the dance club, or theatre company. They were members and they were pursuing allied activities such as lessons and courses to reinforce their arts pursuits. And at the other end of the spectrum, by finding a sub-sample that barely, if at all, registered on our arts involvement scale, we could think of this group as truly non-engaged in the arts and not benefiting directly from things the arts may have to offer.

A. Comparing high-sports and low-sports students.

Our methods for this phase of our analysis of the effects of high involvement in sports during high school directly parallel those used for the arts in Chapter 2. A first step in achieving these comparisons was developing a student-level index of involvement in sports from data available in the NELS database. The indicators related to involvement in sports were the following shown in Figure 3.1.

Figure 3.1 NELS variables used to scale student sports involvement

Grade	NELS Variable Name	NELS Variable Label
Grade 8	BYS82B	PARTICIPATED IN SCHOOL VARSITY SPORTS
Grade 10	F1S8H	NAMED MOST VALUABLE PLAYER ON SPORT TEAM
	F1S41AB	PLAYED BASKETBALL AT SCHOOL
	F1S41AC	PLAYED FOOTBALL AT SCHOOL
	F1S41AD	PLAYED SOCCER AT SCHOOL
	F1S41AE	PARTICIPATED ON SWIM TEAM AT SCHOOL
	F1S41AF	PLAYED OTHER TEAM SPORT
	F1S41AG	PLAYED AN INDIVIDUAL SPORT
	F1S44N	HOW OFTEN R TAKES SPORTS LESSONS
	F1S66F	GOES TO SCHOOL BECAUSE HE PLAYS ON A TEAM
	F1S67B	STUDENTS THINK OF RESPONDENT AS BEING ATHLETIC
	F1S71I	PERSON R ADMIRES MOST IS GOOD AT SPORTS
Grade 12	F2S30AA	PARTICIPATED ON A TEAM SPORT AT SCHOOL
	F2S30AB	PARTICIPATED IN INDIVIDUAL SPORT AT SCHOOL
	F2S33K	HOW OFTEN R TAKES SPORTS LESSONS
	F2S33L	HOW OFTEN DOES R PLAY BALL OR OTH SPORTS
	F2S59D	HOW IMPORTANT IS COLLEGE ATHLETIC PROGRAM

with the arts As with our treatment of the arts variables in NELS, the data for these indicators were scaled in various ways. One common format was a three choice response: participated, did not participate, and participated as a team captain. This scale led to assigning weights of 0 for non participation, 1 for participating, and 3 for participating as a team captain. (Our reasoning for the weight of 3 for captains, as with officers in the band, was that official student leaders are probably the most committed and intensively involved in a discipline, and for the purposes of scaling intensity of involvement, being an official leader was a significant signal.) Another format scaled the amount of involvement, such as 0 for none, 1 for a semester, 2 for a full school year, 3 for three semesters, and 4 for two full school years. We assigned corresponding numbers to responses in this format as contributors to our scale. An analogous format was used for frequency of participation; for how often students took sports lessons, we used (0) for never, (1) for less than once per week, (2) for once per week, (3) for once or twice per week, (4) for almost every day, and so on.

Having created a scaling system for sports involvement, we focused again on the lowest socioeconomic (SES) quartile within the 12,144 students in our full NELS database. This represented about 3000 students whose parents typically had graduated from high school but had engaged in no further education or formal training, or who had themselves dropped out of school without a diploma.

Using this sports involvement scale, we identified the approximately 10 percent of students in this low-SES quartile with the highest sports involvement scale scores, and the 10 percent of students with the lowest scale scores for involvement in sports. Some in this latter group scored simply zero – they showed no detectable participation in athletics in middle school or high school, outside of mandatory physical education classes we should probably say.

We ended up with a high-sports group numbering 323 students and a low-sports group numbering 272 students.

As with the arts in Chapter 2, the group outcome differences we present below are generally expressed as percentages of each group attaining a certain outcome such as finishing college, or comparative percentages of each group participating in a specific activity such as volunteering with youth groups. We focus on indicators of *doing well* as a young adult and we focus on *doing good* as a citizen, particularly on reported participation in various sorts of community service and volunteerism. We also attend to voting in public elections. We attend to student outcomes chronologically, that is showing indications of *doing well* and *doing good* recorded at the age of 20, and then parallel indications generated at the age of 26 – twelve years after the students' first involvement with NELS surveys, tests, and interviews in 8th grade.

What about sports and high-SES students? We again took advantage of the opportunity while performing our data analyses to produce parallel comparisons for the high-SES quartile of students – that is to compare economically advantaged, highly sports-involved students with economically advantaged students who showed little or no engagement in sports on our involvement scale. As with the arts, a first observation generated by a look at the data was the obvious difference in sports participation between students of rich versus poor families. The involved and non-involved low-SES groups were of comparable size, each representing 9 to 10 percent of this quartile. Using the same sports involvement scale score criteria for sorting within the high-income group, the high-SES quartile contained 734 high-sports students (nearly 25 percent of the entire subgroup group) and only 147 low-sports students (about 5 percent of the entire subgroup), as shown in Figure 3.1.2.

> *High-income students were more likely to be highly engaged in sports than low-income students by 19 percent to 10 percent. The imbalance was greater in the arts: 25 percent versus 5 percent of high-SES and low-SES students respectively were highly engaged in the arts.*

Figure 3.1.2

Indicators of early postsecondary education and other activities at age 20, for low SES students, by low and high involvement in secondary school athletics. *Percentages by group.*

		All Students	Hi SES Students		Low SES Students	
N		12144	734	147	323	272
Doing Well			Hi Sports	Low Sports	Hi Sports	Low Sports
Primarily a student in Jan 1994		85.1	97.4	95.4	80.3	79
Sector for first college attended	2-year	29.3	15.2	**22.5**	34.2	30
	4-year	42.3	**80.4**	71.6	25.8	23.2
Doing What?						
Does performing arts		7.5	**12.2**	16.3	4.4	3.4
Participates in sports		49.0	72.1	39.2	**66.5**	41.2
Participates in religious activities		39.6	**45.5**	43.8	42.1	38.7
3 or more hours of TV on weekdays		34.5	24	26.5	43.7	40.9

Bold figures indicate between-group percentage differences significant at p < .05 or better (Chi square, df2 >3.84).

> *In what turns out to be a common story throughout this chapter's analysis of sports engagement in high school, there prove to be fewer differences between sports-engaged and non-sports engaged students than between arts-engaged and non-arts engaged students as far as our indications of doing well and doing good are concerned.*

We first examine the simple comparison – *sports or not*, for both low-income and high-income sub-samples. Then we turn in the following section of this chapter to direct comparisons of arts advantages to sports advantages, and to absolute differences between the effects of high engagement in athletics and high engagement in the arts.

Doing well at age 20, high-sports versus low-sports.

Figure 3.1 shows sports-tied comparisons based on our age 20 *Doing Well* and *Doing What* indicators. For the high versus low-sports-engagement comparisons, few differences emerge. For the low-SES students, having student status at age 20 was about the same for both and very small non-significant differences showed for initial attendance in four-year or two-year colleges. Participation in religious activities and television watching were about the same for the two groups. The only significant difference between the two groups was that 20-year-olds in the low-income group who had been highly engaged in high school sports were about 60 percent more likely to still participate in sports as adults. Early verdict: there is not much difference in *doing well* by age 20 between intense and minimal sports involvement for low-income students. These same sorts of non-differences stand out for high-income students as well.

The main difference attributable to sports engagement applies to both high and low-income groups and is no surprise. Sports interests and skills are likely to carry forward over time; so high-sports students at any income level are likely to show higher sports involvement after leaving high school.

> *The main difference attributable to sports engagement applies to both high and low-income groups and is no surprise. Sports interests and skills are likely to carry forward over time; so high-sports students at any income level are likely to show higher sports involvement after leaving high school.*

In addition, high-SES students from both high and low-sports groups are far more likely than low-SES students to enroll in a four-year college, and high-sports-designated students within the high-SES group are significantly more likely than low-sports students to enter four-year colleges, although both rates are high (about 80 percent versus 72 percent). Rates of 4-year college enrollment were about 25 percent in both low-SES groups. High-SES students in both groups were more likely to still be involved in any sort of formal education at age twenty.

Figure 3.2

Indicators of community service activities at age 20,

by SES and sports involvement groups. Percentages by group.

Doing Good	All Students	Hi SES Students		Low SES Students	
		Hi Sports	Low Sports	Hi Sports	Low Sports
Volunteer work - any	27.9	**38.6**	51.6	**36.0**	27.9
Volunteered at hospitals	10.6	**19.3**	1.0	6.3	7.7
Volunteered, youth orgs, scouts	9.4	**20.2**	8.5	**9.9**	5.3
Vol. sports teams or sports clubs	6.4	**16.4**	3.6	**10.3**	2.5
Vol. church/related (not worship)	11.4	17.1	13.7	12.5	7.7
Vol. educational organizations	6.2	10	12.7	4.4	5.6
Vol. political clubs or organizations	3.1	5.5	5.9	1.8	1.2
Other volunteer work	7.1	8.6	9.5	7.4	6.5
Strong friendships very important	86.0	93.8	91.5	80.1	83.9

Bold figures indicate between-group percentage differences significant at p < .05 or better (Chi square, df2 >3.84).

Figure 3.2 catalogs differences between high and low sports groups on indicators of *doing good*. Seven indicators of specific volunteer or service activities are shown. An overall measure of volunteerism heads the list. And a lone indicator shows percentages of students within groups claiming that strong friendships were very important.

For low-SES students, those highly engaged in sports do more volunteering, about 30 percent more (when we compare a 36 percent rate to a 28 percent rate). Community service differences show significantly in volunteering for youth groups or scouts, and most disproportionately in volunteering for sports teams or sports clubs. These emphases seem reasonable for sports-minded young adult volunteers. For high-SES students, volunteerism among high-sports students extends beyond the youth and sports categories to volunteerism at hospitals. Curiously, among high-SES students, low-sports participants do more volunteering overall (or report doing any volunteering, at least) than the level reported by high-sports participants, by a 52 to 39 percent margin.

In a final analysis, high-sports students in both high and low-income quartiles do more volunteering at age 20 than the average student in NELS (the left-most column), an advantage shown prominently in service to youth and sports organizations.

Doing well at age 26 – high-sports versus low-sports.

Figure 3.3 presents indicators of *doing well* a age 26 – a more extensive set of indicators than we had available or used at age 20. As with the sports-focused statistics presented for age 20 NELS participants, the main story in Figure 3.4 is the absence of significant differences based on sports participation and for many indicators, the lack of much difference at all. An exception is one positive indicator for the low-income high-sports respondents: they are more likely to ever have attended a four-year college (38 percent to 30 percent). But the high-sports group does not score as well on this indicator as the average NELS student. About 54 percent of all students in our total sample attended a four-year college at some point compared to 38 percent of the sports-concentrators from the low-SES quartile.

At both high and low income levels, high-sports students earned lower grades in college than low-sports students, by significant margins.

Figure 3.3

Indicators of higher education and employment-related attainment at age 26,
by SES and sports involvement groups. Percentages by group.

		All Students	Hi SES Students		Low SES Students	
Doing Well			Hi Sports	Low Sports	Hi Sports	Low Sports
Ever attended college after high school		79.1	98.3	97.4	70.6	65.3
Ever attended 4-yr post-sec. institution		53.8	**91.4**	82.7	**37.9**	29.7
Mostly As and Bs as undergraduate		31.0	40.6	**46.1**	17.3	**24.2**
Degree/certificate earned-2000	MA+	3.8	9.7	7.5	1.1	0.3
	BA+	29.6	**72.4**	63.4	13.2	14.8
	ASSOC +	36.9	**77.2**	68.7	22.4	22.5
Holding full time job, 2000		75.3	77.4	71.9	83.8	78
Attending academic institution, 2000		17.5	26.4	23.5	12.1	12.1
Neither work nor academic study, 2000		7.2	0.0	**4.6**	4.1	**9.9**
Dependence on public assistance						
Public aid in 1999		3.1	0.3	0.7	3.7	2.8
Public assistance-food stamps		2.3	0.2	0.3	2.2	2.2

Bold figures indicate between-group percentage differences significant at p < .05 or better (Chi square, df2 >3.84).

completes this assessment of outcomes based on differences in sports participation in high school. Here we present our indicators of *Doing What* – integration sorts of activities as described in Chapter 2 -- and *Doing Good*, captured in a limited number of indicators of service and civic participation.

Once more, in contrast to the series of figures in Chapter 2 showing significant differences between students highly engaged in the arts and those scarcely involved, Figure 3.4 shows few significant differences or advantages for high-sports students. Within the low-income group, the high-sports students are more likely to participate in sports themselves at age 26, and they show higher (but still small) rates of participation in political campaigns (5.5 percent to 2.2

percent). The high-sports students in this group read fewer books.

A few small differences based on sports involvement show up for high-income students. They too read fewer books than their low-sports counterparts, but they read more newspapers and magazines. They are also more likely to participate in sports themselves and to show higher rates of participating as civic or community volunteers.

Figure 3.4

Indicators of activities and community service involvement at age 26, by SES and sports involvement groups. Percentages by group.

Doing What?	All Students	Hi SES Students		Low SES Students	
		Hi Sports	Low Sports	Hi Sports	Low Sports
Read papers or magazines 3+ days/wk.	67.8	**77.9**	69.2	70.2	72.1
Read any books	81	87.6	**94.1**	73.2	**80.2**
Ever go to public library	48.4	47.2	46.4	45.6	48.9
Ever attend plays, concerts	62.4	79.3	76.5	53.7	52.6
Participate in organized religion	56.2	62.1	59.8	58.8	56.3
Participate in sports	46.3	**62.0**	35.9	**64.0**	45.5
Doing Good					
Youth organization volunteer	20	30.2	23.5	20.6	15.5
Civic/community volunteer	21.5	**34.5**	23.2	19.5	15.2
Participate in political campaign	3.6	6.7	5.6	**5.5**	2.2
Registered to vote	76.4	82.2	81.7	75	72.4
Voted in any election, past 24 mos.	41.2	46.4	48.0	34.7	33.8
Voted, 1996 Presidential election (age 22)	55	65.2	65.4	40.8	44.9

Bold figures indicate between-group percentage differences significant at p < .05 or better (Chi square, df2 >3.84).

Finally, in Figure 3.5 we show the indications that the 26-year-olds offered about the value of their postsecondary education and training. There were no significant differences based on sports participation for the low-income group. High-SES students reported that their postsecondary education experiences, which were longer and deeper than those experienced by low-SES students, led to higher paying jobs and to promotion opportunities.

Figure 3.5

Indicators of perceived value of post-secondary education experiences to age 26, by SES and sports involvement groups. Percentages by group.

	All Students	Hi SES Students		Low SES Students	
		Hi Sports	Low Sports	Hi Sports	Low Sports
education has led to better jobs	59.7	84.7	80.7	51.5	45.8
education has led to higher pay	55.2	**81.7**	74.2	45.6	41.8
education has led to more responsibility	60.0	83.8	79.7	53.3	49.2
education leads to promotion opportunity	55.3	**80.7**	73.5	47.1	42.1
aspire to BA+ by age 30	40.4	na	na	32.8	33.6

Bold figures indicate between-group percentage differences significant at p < .05 or better (Chi square, df2 >3.84).

Summing up to this point: high-engagement versus low-engagement in sports

It's fair to say that our run-through of indicators for students highly engaged (versus non-engaged) in high school sports does not produce many appreciable differences between the two groups. The few indicators directly involved with sports, such as continued participation in sports as a young adult, or volunteering with youth sports clubs, do show higher rates of participation for those who had strong sports participation in middle and high school.

In Chapter 2, the arts, in contrast, showed pervasive and systematic differences when we compare highly involved students with low- or non-involved students on our indicators of *doing well* and *doing good*.

It's fair to say that our run-through of indicators for students highly engaged (versus non-engaged) in high school sports does not produce many appreciable differences between the two groups. The arts, in contrast, showed pervasive and systematic differences when we compare highly involved students with low- or non-involved students on our indicators of doing well and doing good. But this is not the full story.

The contrasting patterns shown for the possible effects of sports and arts engagement are cause for thought. The absence of apparent effect in sports could be due to influences we did not attend to. Perhaps something was buoying the prospects of the low-income, low-sports group that rendered these students in fact more like the high sports group in an important way or ways. One such possibility sent us back to our data to check.

What other involvements might our designated non-involved groups have? In particular, we wondered about what members of the low-sports participation groups might have been up to. After all, low participation in one area of high school life leaves room for high participation in others. A quirky possibility occurred to us, not the first time in a research career. What if the low-sports participants tended to be high-arts participants? Based on advantages accruing to arts concentrators suggested in Chapter 2, overpopulation of the low-income, low-sports group by highly arts-involved students might tend to produce the flat results we find for the impacts of sports. This possibility is based on the conjecture that sports do lead to the outcomes suggested by our *doing well* and *doing good* indicators, but that the non-sports students we identified in effect compensated through participation in the arts, or by carrying out other compensatory activities.

A quirky possibility occurred to us, not the first time in a research career. What if the low-sports participants tended to be high-arts participants?

Of course, the possible "other" compensatory activities lay hidden from us, but the arts could be thought of as a promising candidate. If we consider the highly engaged high school student, we do tend to think of athletics of one type or another and the arts of one discipline or another as likely areas to find large numbers of passionately involved students. There are of course a myriad of typically less-subscribed activities that are neither art nor sport: the school newspaper, the annual yearbook, the community service club, the historic train society, and the bird-watchers name a few.

The NELS data are not kind to the prospect of checking out this other-involvement hypothesis, or to testing the specific hypothesis that ignited this thinking. But we did some checking. As things turn out, only 50 of the 272 low-sports, low-income students studied fell into our high-arts group. This 18 percent share might have buoyed outcome measures in the low-sports group marginally, but not enough to suggest that in fact there are differences between high and low-sports groups that our indicators didn't manage to capture. At the same time, only 28 of the 323 low-income, high-sports group classify as low-arts, while 46 classify as high-arts-involved. Any increase in outcome scores this arts presence may have achieved for the high-sports group would probably have been matched by the presence of high-arts students in the low-sports group. Overall, the impact on between-group differences would be miniscule. So much for quirks.

This sub-investigation involved a lot of scurrying back and forth among and across our groups. The possibility seemed plausible. But the low-sports group did not have relatively high scores because they in fact were, unrecognized in the first comparisons, highly involved in the arts instead.

B. How do *arts advantages* and *sports advantages* compare?

In this section we take up a different comparison frame to assess the relative impacts of the arts and sports on our outcome measures. Before going further, the terms advantages or impacts may questioned by readers. We have certainly seen *differentials* for arts, for sports, and between arts and sports. The numbers shown in our indicators or estimates are real – they report what the archived data reflect. But discerning meaning in the numbers is the lion's share of our work and that of scholars more generally. Suggestions that involvement "leads to" things have been offered. The evidence suggests this to be the case – evident differences, passable theory, and consistent data. We have not ruled out rival hypotheses that might explain the data, except for one theory invoking a possible alternatively involved low-sports group to explain non-differences with its counterpart high-sports group.

We proceed here to an additional set of tests. This was standing the arts and sports groups side by side to compare the areas in which concentration in each seems to make a difference. That is, for example, if the arts seem to confer a particular advantage in getting a college degree, how does that compare to the power of sports to inspire the same development?

Figure 3.6

Indicators of early postsecondary education and other activities at age 20, for low SES students, by low and high involvement in secondary school athletics versus arts. Percentages by group.

		All Students		**Low SES Students**			
N		12144	341	316	323	272
Doing Well			*Hi Art*	*Low Art*	*Hi Sports*	*Low Sports*	
Primarily a student in Jan 1994		85.1	80.1	74.8	80.3	79
Sector for first college attended	2-year	29.3	30.5	27.2	34.2	30
	4-year	42.3	29.0	11.4	25.8	23.2
Doing What?						
Does performing arts		7.5	**9.0**	0.3	4.4	3.4
Participates in sports		49.0	39	45.9	**66.5**	41.2
Participates in religious activities		39.6	48.7	34.2	42.1	38.7
3 or more hours of TV on weekdays		34.5	43.1	45.8	43.7	40.9

Focus here is on the high-arts group percentages versus the high-sports group percentages.
Bold figures indicate between-group percentage differences significant at p < .05 or better (Chi square, df2 >3.84).

Figure 3.6 begins this process. Again we concentrate solely on students in the low-income quartile. And the bold indications serve a continuing purpose. They denote significant differences in outcome scores within the arts contrasts and also within the sports contrasts.

This figure shows that advantages for high-arts students were recorded in three areas: enrolling in a four-year college (a more than a 100 percent difference), doing performing arts after high school, and participating in religious activities. High-sports students showed one advantage over low-sports students: more continued participation in sports after high school.

Figure 3.7

Indicators of community service activities at age 20, for low SES students,

by low and high involvement in secondary school athletics versus arts.

	All Students	Low SES Students			
Doing Good		Hi Art	Low Art	Hi Sports	Low Sports
Volunteer work - any	27.9	**37.2**	19.6	**36.0**	27.9
Volunteered at hospitals	10.6	**7.9**	4.1	6.3	7.7
Volunteered, youth orgs, scouts	9.4	**7.9**	3.2	**9.9**	5.3
Vol. sports teams or sports clubs	6.4	4.1	2.5	**10.3**	2.5
Vol. church/related (not worship)	11.4	**16.7**	7.3	12.5	7.7
Vol. educational organizations	6.2	**5.9**	1.4	4.4	5.6
Vol. political clubs or organizations	3.1	2.7	1.0	1.8	1.2
Other volunteer work	7.1	**7.6**	3.5	7.4	6.5
Strong friendships very important	86.0	**82.4**	75.3	80.1	83.9

Bold figures indicate between-group percentage differences significant at p < .05 or better (Chi square, df2 >3.84).

Figure 3.7 shows *doing good* indicators at age 20. The general story in this figure is that in a head to head comparison between high-arts and high-sports students, there is little significant difference. The high-sports students do volunteer significantly more with sports teams and sports clubs than the high-arts students. The arts students show a possible advantage in church-related voluntarism. Otherwise, the percentages in each group for each indicator are very close.

Doing Well at Age 26

As shown in Figure 3.8, being highly engaged in the arts in secondary school pays off in nine areas that we have inventoried among our *Doing Well* indicators at age 26. These include the full array of educational attainment and achieve-

Figure 3.8

Indicators of higher education and employment-related attainment at age 26, for low SES students, by low and high involvement in secondary school athletics versus arts.

Doing Well		All Students	Low SES Students			
			Hi Art	Low Art	Hi Sports	Low Sports
Ever attended college after high school		79.1	**70.7**	48.1	70.6	65.3
Ever attended 4-yr post-sec. institution		53.8	**38.7**	16.8	**37.9**	29.7
Mostly As and Bs as undergraduate		31.0	**14.7**	8.5	17.3	**24.2**
Degree/certificate earned-2000	MA+	3.8	**0.8**	0.3	1.1	0.3
	BA+	29.6	**17.7**	6.3	13.2	14.8
	Assoc +	36.9	**24.0**	10.3	22.4	22.5
Holding full time job, 2000		75.3	75.1	69.3	83.8	78
Attending academic institution, 2000		17.5	**11.7**	6.6	12.1	12.1
Neither work nor academic study, 2000		7.2	13.2	**24.1**	4.1	**9.9**
Dependence on public assistance						
Public aid in 1999		3.1	4.1	**8.5**	3.7	2.8
Public assistance-food stamps		2.3	2.9	**7.9**	2.2	2.2

Bold figures indicate between-group percentage differences significant at p < .05 or better (Chi square, df2 >3.84).

ment indicators – from getting better grades to earning more and higher-level college degrees. For instance, the 17.7 percent of the high-arts sample had earned bachelors degrees or higher by age 26; only 6.3 percent of the low-arts group did so. The figure also shows that across the nation, for students at all income levels, that 29.6 percent had earned bachelors degrees or higher. Suppressing effects of low family income are quite evident in these data. The low-SES groups was more than twice as likely to be depending on public assistance at age 26, when compared to the average students.

Having high-sports versus low-sports engagement in high school produces one important advantage among these *doing well* indicators, namely the likelihood of ever attending a 4-year college (37.9 versus 29.7 percent). All except one of the remaining academic indicators show no differences by sports engagement status. The exception is that sports concentrators earn lower grades in college – by about one-third.

Figure 3.9

Indicators of activities and community service involvement at age 26, for low by low and high involvement in secondary school athletics versus arts.

Doing What?	All Students	Hi Art	Low Art	Hi Sports	Low Sports
Read papers or magazines 3+ days/wk.	67.8	76.5	75.0	70.2	72.1
Read any books	81	**81.8**	73.8	73.2	**80.2**
Ever go to public library	48.4	**55.1**	43.0	45.6	48.9
Ever attend plays, concerts	62.4	56.4	48.1	53.7	52.6
Participate in organized religion	56.2	**64.8**	47.8	58.8	56.3
Participate in sports	46.3	44.1	41.1	**64.0**	45.5
Doing Good					
Youth organization volunteer	20	**24.3**	10.8	20.6	15.5
Civic/community volunteer	21.5	**24.6**	10.4	19.5	15.2
Participate in political campaign	3.6	4.1	2.8	**5.5**	2.2
Registered to vote	76.4	**77.7**	67.1	75	72.4
Voted in any election, past 24 mos.	41.2	37	30.4	34.7	33.8
Voted, 1996 Presidential election (age 22)	55	**52.5**	35.1	40.8	44.9

Bold figures indicate between-group percentage differences significant at p < .05 or better (Chi square, df2 >3.84).

Figure 3.9 continues with age-26 indicators for doing integrative sorts of activities (*doing what*) and also our indicators of *doing good*. Here we see a number of advantages for the high- as opposed to low-arts group, and only two material differences across the sports groups. In sports, the high-sports students participate in sports at age 26 more frequently than the low-sports students. High-sports students report reading fewer books than non-sports students. When comparing high- and low-arts groups at age 26, advantages favoring the high-arts group show in more than half of all indicators. These include more reading books, going to the library, participation in organized religion, youth and civic volunteering, and voting behavior.

Summing up. A count of areas where high-arts or high-sports students, versus their low involvement counterparts, supports one appraisal of the comparative effects of the arts versus sports in promoting positive developments. In this case, the arts show as stronger. In comparison to low-arts students, the high-arts students show significant advantages in 30 out of 44 indicators of *doing well* and *doing good* at ages 20 and 26. In comparison, high-sports status versus low-sports status associates with only 7 significant advantages.

> *If the critical criterion is a count of areas where high-arts or high-sports matter, high-arts status shows significant advantages in 30 out of our 44 indicators of Doing Well and Doing Good at ages 20 and 26. In comparison, high-sports status versus low-sports status associates with only 7 statistically significant advantages.*

Through this point in the analysis, it appears that intensive engagement in the arts may have more advantages for low-income middle and high school youth than does involvement in athletics. But the whole story is not written in these data. We now turn to another way of framing the arts versus sports question.

Comparing High-arts with High-sports directly.

In this analysis, we use the same data presented the previous section and ask a different question. This is whether or not there are differences between high-arts and high-sports groups in absolute levels of success across our indicators--

such as, how do high-sports and high-arts groups compare on percentages entering four-year colleges, or on overall participation in community service. As readers will see, this becomes a matter of comparing just two columns in the previous tables (high-sports and high-arts figures) and testing for significant differences.

Figure 3.10

Indicators of early postsecondary education and other activities at age 20, for low SES students, by low and high involvement in secondary school athletics versus arts. Percentages by group.

		All Students		Low SES Students			
	N	12144	341	316	323	272
Doing Well			*Hi Art*	*Low Art*	*Hi Sports*	*Low Sports*
Primarily a student in Jan 1994		85.1	80.1	75	80.3	79
Sector for first college attended	2-year	29.3	30.5	27.2	34.2	30
	4-year	42.3	29.0	11.4	25.8	23.2
Doing What?						
Does performing arts		7.5	**9.0**	0.3	4.4	3.4
Participates in sports		49.0	39	45.9	**66.5**	41.2
Participates in religious activities		39.6	48.7	34.2	42.1	38.7
3 or more hours of TV on weekdays		34.5	43.1	45.8	43.7	40.9

Focus here is on the shaded columns -- the high-arts group percentages versus the high-sports group percentages.
Bold figures indicate between-group percentage differences significant at $p < .05$ or better (Chi square, df2 >3.84).

Figure 3.10 begins our report of this analysis. Here a bold indication in either the Hi Art or Hi Sports column shows that a statistically significant difference exists between that and the corresponding figure for the other discipline. As an example, two large differences between sports and arts show here. Nearly two-thirds (66.5 percent) of high-sports students still participate in sports at age 20. Only 39 percent of high-arts students do so. These two percentages differ significantly and so the larger is entered in bold. And flipping this situation around, nine percent of high art students report involvement in the performing arts at age 20. The corresponding rate for high sport students in only 4.4 percent. Thus the statistic **9.0** shows in bold. These data suggest continuity of sports and arts interests beyond high school. They also show that among school-based enthusiasts, participation in sports activities carries over beyond high school in much larger numbers than does arts participation.

Figure 3.11

Indicators of community service activities at age 20, for low SES students,

by low and high involvement in secondary school athletics versus arts.

Doing Good		All Students	Hi Art	Low Art	Hi Sports	Low Sports
Volunteer work - any		27.9	**37.2**	19.6	**36.0**	27.9
Volunteered at hospitals		10.6	**7.9**	4.1	6.3	7.7
Volunteered, youth orgs, scouts		9.4	**7.9**	3.2	**9.9**	5.3
Vol. sports teams or sports clubs		6.4	4.1	2.5	**10.3**	2.5
Vol. church/related (not worship)		11.4	**16.7**	7.3	12.5	7.7
Vol. educational organizations		6.2	**5.9**	1.4	4.4	5.6
Vol. political clubs or organizations		3.1	2.7	1.0	1.8	1.2
Other volunteer work		7.1	**7.6**	3.5	7.4	6.5
Strong friendships very important		86.0	**82.4**	75.3	80.1	83.9

Bold figures indicate between-group percentage differences significant at p < .05 or better (Chi square, df2 >3.84).

Figure 3.11 shows comparisons for *doing good* between sports and arts concentrators at age 20. The main story in this figure is its absence of significant differences when comparing the high-sports and high-arts students. More than a third of both groups do some volunteering, 8 percent to 10 percent volunteer with youth organizations, and practically no one in either group volunteers with political clubs and organizations (fewer than 2 percent in both). The one meaningful difference shows in volunteering with sports teams and sports clubs – more frequently done by members of the high-sports group.

Figure 3.12

Indicators of higher education and employment-related attainment at age 26, for low SES students, by low and high involvement in secondary school athletics versus arts.

		All Students	Hi Art	Low Art	Hi Sports	Low Sports
					Low SES Students	
Doing Well						
Ever attended college after high school		79.1	**70.7**	48.1	70.6	65.3
Ever attended 4-yr post-sec. institution		53.8	**38.7**	16.8	**37.9**	29.7
Mostly As and Bs as undergraduate		31.0	**14.7**	8.5	17.3	**24.2**
Degree/certificate earned-2000	MA+	3.8	**0.8**	0.3	1.1	0.3
	BA+	29.6	**17.7**	6.3	13.2	14.8
	Assoc +	36.9	**24.0**	10.3	22.4	22.5
Holding full time job, 2000		75.3	75.1	69.3	83.8	78
Attending academic institution, 2000		17.5	**11.7**	6.6	12.1	12.1
Neither work nor academic study, 2000		7.2	13.2	**24.1**	4.1	**9.9**
Dependence on public assistance						
Public aid in 1999		3.1	4.1	**8.5**	3.7	2.8
Public assistance-food stamps		2.3	2.9	**7.9**	2.2	2.2

Bold figures indicate between-group percentage differences significant at p < .05 or better (Chi square, df2 >3.84).

As shown in Figure 3.12, at age 26, the comparisons continue to show little difference between the success rates of the two groups. About 70 percent of both groups attended some college after high school, about 38 percent of both enrolled initially in four-year colleges, college grades were about the same, and dependence on public assistance was low and similar for the two groups.

Figure 3.13

*Indicators of activities and community service involvement at age 26, for lov
by low and high involvement in secondary school athletics versus arts.*

	All Students	Low SES Students			
Doing What?		Hi Art	Low Art	Hi Sports	Low Sports
Read papers or magazines 3+ days/wk.	67.8	76.5	75.0	70.2	72.1
Read any books	81	**81.8**	73.8	73.2	**80.2**
Ever go to public library	48.4	**55.1**	43.0	45.6	48.9
Ever attend plays, concerts	62.4	56.4	48.1	53.7	52.6
Participate in organized religion	56.2	**64.8**	47.8	58.8	56.3
Participate in sports	46.3	44.1	41.1	**64.0**	45.5
Doing Good					
Youth organization volunteer	20	**24.3**	10.8	20.6	15.5
Civic/community volunteer	21.5	**24.6**	10.4	19.5	15.2
Participate in political campaign	3.6	4.1	2.8	**5.5**	2.2
Registered to vote	76.4	**77.7**	67.1	75	72.4
Voted in any election, past 24 mos.	41.2	37	30.4	34.7	33.8
Voted, 1996 Presidential election (age 22)	55	**52.5**	35.1	40.8	44.9

Bold figures indicate between-group percentage differences significant at p < .05 or better (Chi square, df2 >3.84).

At age 26, the comparisons between arts and sports begin to
differentiate. The one sort of advantage shown for sports-rich
students maintains. They are more likely to continue
participation in sports by 64 percent to 44 percent – a nearly
50 percent difference. Given the prominence of advice to
adults to exercise regularly from medical and other quarters,
this advantage shown for students highly engaged in high
school sports might be considered very valuable. We will
have to wait for the NELS age 60 panel to find out!

The arts-involved group shows a set of advantages over the
high-sports group in measures associated with reading –
reading newspapers or magazines, reading books, and
patronizing public libraries. Rates in the reading categories
are high for both groups, 70 to 73 percent in the sports group

and 77 to 82 percent in the arts group. Library attendance is lower, 46 percent for the sports group and 55 percent for the arts group.

We are tempted to offer a spurious pronouncement here. The advantages in adult health conferred by high involvement in sports in high school and continued exercise into adulthood might be balanced out by higher incidence of reading helpful advice about health care and healthy living in adulthood by the high-arts group. But that would be going beyond the data.

> *High-sports students are more likely than high-arts students to be participating in sports at age 26. The arts students are more likely to read books and magazines and be found at the library at the same age. (Perhaps one group will sustain adult health though exercise. The other will sustain health by acting on written information and advice!)*

Summing up. In the side-by-side direct comparisons of our low-income high-arts and high-sports groups, the patterns should be considered equivalent. Arts-intensive and sport-intensive low-income youth show similar success levels in postsecondary education and in serving others while in college and while working beyond high school, that is, of *doing well* and *doing good*. So both conditions can be said to matter; when the arts group is compared to its low-arts comparison group, and the sports group to its comparison, the arts can be said to matter more. This is a framing question.

Comparing arts and sports groups to completely uninvolved students.

We raised an issue earlier that we want to push harder on before we close this chapter. This was our lack of knowledge of the circumstances of our two low-involvement groups – the low-arts and low-sports students – when we used them as baseline groups. While there is reason to think that students in each of these groups may be actively engaged in what their schools had to offer, their lack of engagement in our respective groups could be met by high engagement in something else. One possibility was high art involvement within the low-sports group; we checked and this was not an issue. Or our low-arts group may have had high-sports involvement, a possibility we did not investigate.

We turn to now to a final test concerned with the non-involvement groups we used. How did the sports and arts students do when compared to student with very low involvement scores in both the arts and sports? The questions here become high-arts versus no appreciable involvement of any sort, and high-sports versus no appreciable involvement of any sort. (We assume that significant numbers of students lacking involvement in either arts or sports would actually be low-involvement *overall*.) This new comparison group would almost certainly be less involved in high school on average than either of the low-involvement groups we have studied. The comparison we are trying to make, then, is doing art as opposed to doing nothing; or doing sports versus doing nothing.

> *The comparison we are trying to make is doing visual and performing arts as opposed to little engagement of any sort in school; or doing sports as opposed to little engagement at all.*

✳ ✳ ✳

Figure 3.14 Comparing High Art and High Sports Students to Students Low in Both Art and Sport, Age 20

	N	12441	341	323	295
Doing Well -- Age 20		**All Students**	**_Hi Art_**	**_Hi Sports_**	**Low in Arts and Sports**
Current activity full time job		75.3	69.3	78	77.3
Sector for first college attended	2-year	29.3	30.5	34.2	29.8
	4-year	42.3	**29.0**	**25.8**	15.3
Doing What -- Age 20					
Does performing arts		7.5	**9.0**	4.4	3.6
Participates in sports		49.0	39	**66.5**	42.7
Participates in religious activities		39.6	**48.7**	**42.1**	35.9
3 or more hours of TV on weekdays		34.5	43.1	43.7	42.3

Doing Good -- Age 20		**_Hi Art_**	**_Hi Sports_**	**Low in Arts and Sports**
Volunteer work - any	27.9	**37.2**	**36.0**	25.8
Volunteered at hospitals	10.6	**7.9**	6.3	5.4
Volunteered, youth orgs, scouts	9.4	**7.9**	**9.9**	4.4
Vol. sports teams or sports clubs	6.4	4.1	**10.3**	2.0
Vol. church/related (not worship)	11.4	**16.7**	12.5	10.2
Vol. educational organizations	6.2	5.9	4.4	4.7
Vol. political clubs or organizations	3.1	2.7	1.8	1.7
Other volunteer work	7.1	**7.6**	**7.4**	4.1
Strong friendships very important	86.0	82.4	80.1	80.3

Bold figures indicate advantages for students in high-arts or high-sports groups when compared to non-involved students (right column); percentage differences significant at p < .05, Chi Square df2 > 3.84.

3.14 displays outcome statistics for the low-income, high-arts students and the overall non-engaged low-income students at age 20. It also shows statistics for the high-sports students. The bold indications do not reflect differences between art and sport-focused students. The bold indications rather show significant differences between the indicated group and the general low-involvement students in the right column. Where both arts and sports show as bold figures, their scores are both significantly higher than those in the right column – the scores of the non-involved group. In some cases, only the arts show a bolded entry or only sports does so; these are instances where one and not the other shows a significant difference between its pursuits and "doing nothing."

Both sports and arts show advantages over doing little or nothing – in increasing access to 4-year colleges (with an edge for the arts group) and participating in volunteer activities generally. Both arts and sports groups participated more often in religion, with an edge to the arts group.

The arts-involved students are more likely to be found doing performing arts after high school as well as volunteering at hospitals and churches. The sports-involved students are more likely to be found participating in sports and volunteering for sports clubs.

Age 26 differences

As shown in Figure 3.15, high-arts and high-sports students show similar profiles in *doing well* and *doing good* in comparison to what we gauge to be the *largely uninvolved* high school student. (Although we have not shown that involvement levels in this latter group are typically nil, we suspect this comparison group has very low overall levels of engagement in extracurricular activities.)

Both the arts and sports groups depart significantly from non-engaged students on beliefs that their postsecondary education has benefited them in the job market, both groups outstrip non-involved students in voting behavior – registering and voting. Both groups also surpass the non-involved in all volunteering activities; and both show lower levels of dependence on public assistance as of age 26.

The high-sports group maintains its ever-present tendency to produce active participation in sports beyond high school.

Figure 3.15 Comparing High Art and High Sports Students to Students Low in Both Art and Sports, Age 26

Doing Well -- Age 26		*All Students*	*Hi Art*	*Hi Sports*	*Low in Arts and Sports*
Ever attended college after high school		79.1	**70.7**	**70.6**	55.6
Ever attended 4-yr post-sec. institution		53.8	**38.7**	**37.9**	22.4
Mostly As and Bs as undergraduate		31.0	14.7	17.3	_15.9_
Degree/certificate earned-2000	MA+	3.8	0.8	1.1	0.7
	BA+	29.6	_17.7_	13.2	10.9
	Assoc +	36.9	24.0	22.4	26.6
Holding full time job, 2000		75.3	75.1	83.8	77.3
Attending academic institution, 2000		17.5	11.7	12.1	9.2
Dependence on public assistance					
Public aid in 1999		3.1	4.1	3.7	5.8
Public assistance-food stamps		2.3	**2.9**	**2.2**	5.1

Doing What -- Age 26			*Hi Art*	*Hi Sports*	*Low in Arts and Sports*
Read papers or magazines 3+ days/wk.		67.8	**76.5**	70.2	66.5
Read any books		81	**81.8**	73.2	36.7
Ever go to public library		48.4	**55.1**	45.6	47.5
Ever attend plays, concerts		62.4	**56.4**	53.7	47.8
Participate in organized religion		56.2	**64.8**	58.8	51.5
Participate in sports		46.3	44.1	**64.0**	45.4

Doing Good -- Age 26			*Hi Art*	*Hi Sports*	*Low in Arts and Sports*
Youth organization volunteer		20	**24.3**	**20.6**	14.2
Civic/community volunteer		21.5	**24.6**	**19.5**	11.2
Participate in political campaign		3.6	**4.1**	**5.5**	1.7
Registered to vote		76.4	**77.7**	**75**	53.9
Voted in any election, past 24 mos.		41.2	37	34.7	33.9
Voted, 1996 Pres. election (age 22)		55	**52.5**	**40.8**	29.5

			Hi Art	*Hi Sports*	*Low in Arts and Sports*
education has led to better jobs		59.7	**50.7**	**51.5**	38.6
education has led to higher pay		55.2	45.2	45.6	37.3
education has led to more responsibility		60.0	**54.5**	**53.3**	41.7
education leads to promotion oppt'y.		55.3	**48.1**	**47.1**	38.6
aspire to BA+ by age 30		40.4	36.7	32.8	31.2

Bold figures indicate between-group differences significant at p < .05 or better (Chi square, df2 >3.84).
Underscored percentage figures are suggestive advantages but not significant (Chi square, df2 <3.84).

And the high-arts group again shows a comparative advantage when it comes to reading books and magazines and frequenting the library. Two additional advantages for an arts-involved high school career emerge: increased attendance at concerts and plays, and higher participation in organized religion.

Summing up. This final exercise sets each of the arts and sports group up against an important comparison condition – students with very low indicated involvement in anything during high school. All students assessed were in the low-SES quartile, as was typical for most our analyses. We chose these comparison students because they qualified as both low-arts and low-sports students. That is, they were in the bottom ten percent of our participation scales in both areas.

An overall impression obtained from the results is that both the arts and sports confer benefits when pursued in middle and high school. Sports involvement has an edge when it comes to promoting adult involvement in sports; no surprise there. Arts involvement shows an edge when it comes to several personal pursuits – reading books and magazines, (activities with some academic flavor), and increased participation in the arts as young adults. For reasons that seem important if only because of the consistency of this pattern, across many ways of looking at arts involvement, art connects to participation in religion and service to religious organizations. As far as religious participation goes, the indicators frequently approach 25 percent in high-arts contexts and just about always outpace comparison groups – low-arts students, low-sports students, high-sports students, all low-income students and the completely or nearly-completely non-involved.

Choice among passions. When we first entertained questions about whether we were studying art or studying engagement, our thinking was that there would be similarities between engagement in the arts and engagement in other high school activities. This impression holds up for the ubiquitous question about sports. This thinking was based on research about the importance of engagement with schools and colleges and with institutions more generally.

Taking an engagement hypothesis another step, we would assert that students will differ widely in the interests they wish to pursue as secondary students, in their abilities to find resources and locate channels to support what they want to do, and that students are not necessarily interchangeable when it comes to their passions. The varsity basketball player may be a miserable fish out of water if placed in the school play, and/or ill-equipped to join the orchestra. At the same time, the gifted sketch-artist, painter, or dance choreographer would be out of place if assigned to the wrestling team (although there could be reason to bet on the choreographer if muscle tone and stamina mattered). Of course these are not descriptions of meaningful experiments – each of these students has come to his and interests over a period of time, often long-rooted in early learning experiences as well as school and out-of-school experiences.

What may be a most import implication of this analysis is that students stand to benefit from opportunities to choose among passions in school – and to arrive at the middle or high school door with a good range of ways to become engaged in the institution.

Optimum match. The work of Professor Jacqueline Eccles, a psychologist who has turned her extensive experience and skill in motivation-related measurement to youth engagement, and who has published a number of studies related to extracurricular activities in high school, suggests one way of thinking about how we conceive engagement. She points to the importance of the "goodness of fit" between the student and the activity. She is interested in the developments and skills when people act in roles that can capitalize on their individual skills. Or optimizing the match between the student and his environment. Her work provides evidence that a good fit will produce more positive outcomes than just participation *per se*. Another way the learning psychology profession describes this kind of relationship is this: the effects of *ability-environment interaction* tends to outweigh the effects of individual differences between students (such as their abilities) or the effects of circumstances surrounding students (such as they types of schools or extracurricular activities they find themselves in).[xxxv]

So what we have been comparing in many ways can be thought of students who have found a fit with arts, and students who have found a fit with sports. But we have to return to Chapter 2 and remind ourselves of its arguments and findings. The arts do matter in a number of important ways – in leading to positive academic outcomes as well as to lives where we contribute to the welfare of others. The arts matter for those who become engaged in the arts. The arts are a productive path. One among many for our youth, but one where some children will find their optimum match, or a good fit between themselves and the pursuit, or a chance to maximize the benefits of Eccles' *ability-environment* interaction.

Passions that matter, passions encouraged for children, passions met with resources necessary for engagement. These seem the central issues when it comes to arts education. We've provided evidence that the arts lead to positive outcomes. The arts should stand before children as passions they can freely choose.

Chapter 4

The *Curve of Binding Artistic Energy*: Arts-rich versus arts-poor schools

Testing ideas that ethos and belief within cohesive arts-focused schools make a difference.

Introduction

A few research studies in recent years have approached the potential importance of the arts in secondary education from a standpoint departing from the approach we used and report in our first three chapters. This research tracks questions about the importance of multi-arts experiences, which is consistent with how we defined high-arts involvement for our students. In a related vein, some efforts investigate what should be called the potential value of *arts-rich* schools. The focus of these inquiries goes beyond possible direct effects of the arts on academic or social development; the questions of interest probe possibilities that very art-rich schools develop cultures in which assumptions and attitudes about children and learning take on distinct, productive qualities -- and whether arts-rich schools develop strong and positive links with their student families and wider external communities that assist in their effectiveness. One way to put what researchers here wonder is whether arts-rich schools become truly special places where all students are more likely to have good learning experiences and to develop strong interpersonal relationships, social bonds, and values. These questions can be informed by reasonably up-close examination and assessment of schools in action, and that is just what several good studies have managed to do.

A recent study undertaken by the Arts Education Partnership under sponsorship by the Ford Foundation explored arts-rich

schools in the USA, with in-depth, long-term studies in ten elementary and secondary schools selected for their success beyond expectations inferred from their high poverty family conditions and at-risk community settings. This was a three-year study that explored the effects of an arts-centered curriculum on school improvement. Titled *Third Space: When Learning Matters*, the research enlisted this term as "...a metaphor that describes the positive and supportive relationships that develop among students, teachers and the school community when they are involved in creating, performing or responding to works of art. It is the place where connections get made." The authors found that, "...the arts play an important role in changing education and encouraging new thinking about teaching and learning." And moreover, they reported, "For many students, where school had often been a place of failure and frustration, the experience of success in the arts was a revelation that learning matters – and that they themselves matter."[xxxvi]

In addition, an evaluation of the A+ Schools program drew together a common denominator of the research on art-rich schools in their finding that the A+ schools developed a "coherent arts-based identity."[xxxvii] Coherence is central and important to the observations in these studies. Coherent school programs make sense to their constituents, coherent programs contain elements that work to reinforce each other rather than stand in opposition, and coherent programs are infused with sets of values that participants share and feel are vital to the work of education. These schools exhibited a shared sense of purpose and common visions for the students and organizational futures.

Exploring arts-rich schools in NELS.

The studies cited above were done in modest samples of schools and relied on retrospective, contemporaneous, and to a limited degree longitudinal views of events and outcomes in the schools. The NELS survey presents a 12-year developmental arc and permits an unprecedented assessment of arts-rich schools. NELS also supports quantitative conceptions of arts infusion that can be applied to its sample of 1000 schools; and which helps to locate schools that should be called arts-poor or arts-barren by comparison.

NELS supports an examination of long-term outcomes for students who attend arts-rich schools in comparison to arts-poor schools. We used available information about the NELS schools that indicate the schools' interest and involvement in the arts – not necessarily the arts engagement of the students. These variables are shown in Table 4.1. They include availability of various arts programs, whether or not a school requires music or art for graduation, whether the school has a formal department of art and/or of music, and the number of arts and music faculty. For the faculty counts, we used a ratio of full-time arts faculty to full-time English faculty to adjust for school size.

The next step should sound familiar. We developed a scale of arts-richness based on individual school scores and isolated the top and bottom ten percent of schools on this scale. We call these arts-rich and arts-poor schools. The arts-rich schools so identified are almost certain to look more like the *Third Space* or *A+* schools introduced above than are our arts-poor schools. At the same time, it is no doubt possible to score at the high ranges on our arts-rich scale and not exhibit the *zeitgeist* or cohesion of the schools praised in recent research. A school could score poorly on our arts-rich scale and yet be wholly an arts-rich school according to everything we might wish for such an institution. A school massively infused with a dance program (or any single-focus) program, one that had students, parents, teachers, and faculty completely absorbed and that sent its graduates to Juilliard, the School of the American Ballet Theatre, and apprenticeships with Twyla Tharp or Merce Cunningham might easily look like an arts-poor school on our homely scale. This is because they may lack a band or orchestra and a music or arts department, and have no graduation requirements in any art. This problem with scaling from these sorts of variables constitutes powerful arguments for research that involves long-term researcher presence in the participating schools. But it's hard to have things both ways – a broad array of information on institutions and students that is consistent, standardized, and countable – or rich, contextualized, and idiosyncratic information based on up-close observation and interaction with research sites and subjects.

Table 4.1   NELS Variables used to scale arts-rich / arts-poor schools

Grade	Variable Name	Variable Label
Grade 10	F1C70H	GRADUATION REQUIREMENTS FOR ART
	F1C70I	GRADUATION REQUIREMENTS FOR MUSIC
	F1C71B	BAND/ORCHESTRA AVAILABLE IN 10TH GRADE
	F1C71C	CHORUS OR CHOIR AVAILABLE IN 10TH GRADE
	F1C71E	DRAMA CLUB(S) AVAILABLE IN 10TH GRADE
	F1C71P	ORCHESTRA AVAILABLE TO 10TH GR. STUDNTS
Grade 12	F2C35C	FORMAL DEPT - ART
	F2C35D	FORMAL DEPT - MUSIC
	F2C36C1	NUMBER OF FULL-TIME ART FACULTY MEMBERS
	F2C36D1	NUMBER OF FULL-TIME MUSIC FACULTY

How we proceeded. We are very brief here, because we proceeded in the same way we went about our work in the previous chapters. Our task here was to examine the outcomes for low-income (bottom SES quartile) students who attended either arts-rich (top decile) or arts-poor (bottom decile) schools. We also wanted to explore outcomes in our now-familiar structure, *doing well* and *doing good* respectively at age 20 and age 26.

Doing Well and *Doing Good* at age 20, arts-rich vs. arts-poor schools.

Figure 4.1 shows *doing well* outcome indicators for low-income students attending arts-rich versus arts-poor high schools.

Figure 4.1. ARTS RICH vs. ARTS POOR HIGH SCHOOLS

Education Attainments and Other Activities, Age 20.
Low SES students

Indicators of early postsecondary education and other activities at age 20, for low SES students, by attendance at arts rich versus arts poor high schools. Percentages by group.

		All Students		**Low SES Students**	
	N	12144		268	368
Doing Well		school type>>		*Arts Rich*	*Arts Poor*
Primarily a student in Jan 1994		85.1	x	**79.4**	70.1
Sector for first college attended	2-year	29.3		28.7	31.3
	4-year	42.3	x	**37.7**	24.7
Pursuing BA at age 20		35.6	x	**29.1**	17.7
Pursuing Associate degree		15.7	x	20.5	17.7
Involved in some post-sec. education		68.8		**45.9**	34.0
BA or higher expected		68.8	x	64.5	58.9
MA or higher expected		37.8		30.2	23.0
Doing What					
Does performing arts		7.5		4.9	5.2
2 or fewer hours of TV on weekdays		65.5	x	61.6	57.3
Registered to vote, age 20		70.2	x	72.4	65.8
Voted in 1992 Presidential election		47.6	x	**47.0**	38.6
			(*)		

Bold figures indicate between-group percentage differences significant at p < .05 or better (N 368/268. Chi square, df2 >3.84).
(*) X = comparison favors arch rich schools, some not statistically significant.

The most prominent and important differences for the arts-rich school students are in academic domains following high school. These include a 14 percent higher probability of being a student in some post-secondary environment (colleges and trade-schools, full or part time) at age 20 and a 50 percent higher likelihood of pursuing a BA degree at the same age. A difference also significant lies in enrollment in colleges.

Doing good indicators for age 20 are displayed in Figure 4.2.

Few specific differences stand out in this figure, except in the first important element. Students attending arts-rich schools were more likely to report involvement in any volunteer work at age 20, by about 36 to 28 percent. It is worth pointing out that the arts-rich students score higher than the average student in all of NELS on this indicator of voluntarism (shown in the leftmost column). Across the integrative activities shown, only one difference stood out, the increased likelihood to have voted in the recent presidential election for the arts-rich students. This is another indicator where the students from arts-rich schools match the average student in performance or participation. And in saying this, we must remember that the All Students category contains students from all four SES quartiles, and not just the poorest. That the 1992 election was something of a watershed in our nation's political saga (W.J. Clinton turning G.H.W. Bush into a one-term President) might have ties to our statistics.

Figure 4.2. ARTS RICH vs. ARTS POOR HIGH SCHOOLS

**Community service activities at age 20,
Low SES students**

Doing Good		All Students		Low SES Students	
	N	12144		268	368
		school type>>		Arts Rich	Arts Poor
Volunteer work - any		27.9	x	**35.9**	27.6
Volunteered at hospitals		10.6	x	6.1	5.3
Volunteered, youth orgs, scouts		9.4	x	5.0	3.6
Vol. sports teams or sports clubs		6.4	x	4.9	4.3
Vol. church/related (not worship)		11.4		9.7	14.1
Vol. educational organizations		6.2	x	4.5	3.3
Vol. political clubs or organizations		3.1	x	3.4	2.4
Other volunteer work		7.1		4.1	6.3
Strong friendships very important		92.4	x	87.7	82.3
Registered to vote, age 20		70.2	x	72.4	65.8
Voted in 1992 Presidential election		47.6	x	**47**	38.6
			(*)		

Bold figures indicate between-group percentage differences significant at p < .05 or better (N 368/268. Chi square, df2 >3.84).

(*) X = comparison favors arch rich schools, some not statistically significant.

Doing well at Age 26

Indicators of *doing well* for students attending arts-rich schools are displayed in the next table, Figure 4.3.

Figure 4.3. Arts Rich vs. Arts Poor Schools

Indicators of higher education and employment-related attainment at age 26, by attendance at arts rich versus arts poor high schools. Percentages by group.

Low SES students

A. Doing Well		All Students		Low SES Students	
	N	12144		268	368
		school type>>		Arts Rich	Arts Poor
Ever attended college after high school		79.1	x	**78.7**	67.1
Ever attended 4 year college		53.8	x	**48.9**	33.2
Mostly As and Bs as undergraduate		31.0	x	**29.1**	20.2
Degrees earned as of age 26	MA+	3.8	x	2.6	0.8
	BA+	29.6	x	**25**	11.7
	AA+	36.9	x	**38.8**	20.9
Holding full time job as of 2000		75.3	x	75.7	74.2
Attending academic institution, 2000		17.5	x	18.7	18.5
Received public assistance in 1999		3.1	x	1.1	**5.4**
Education has led to better jobs		59.7	x	**58.2**	43.5
Education has led to higher pay		55.2	x	**53.4**	39.7
Education has led to more responsibility		60.0	x	**59**	47
Education leads to promotion opportunity		55.3	x	**54.1**	40.5
Read any books		81	x	**81.8**	73.8
Ever go to public library		48.4	x	**55.1**	43.0
Ever attend plays, concerts		62.4	x	**56.4**	48.1
Ever participate in sports		53.7		42.9	50.3

Bold figures indicate between-group percentage differences significant at p < .05 or better (N 368/268. Chi square, df2 >3.84).

(*) X = comparison favors arch rich schools, some not statistically significant.

In this display, a great many indicators of advantage appear for students of arts-rich schools. In fact most categories show statistically significant differences for the arts-rich school participants. A full survey of Figure 4.3 shows that the advantages form a cluster that can be described as increased educational attainment and achievement. Sizeable differences show in ever attending college after high school, ever attending a 4-year college, earning a BA (a more than 100 percent advantage here), and in attaining associate degrees.

A great many indicators of advantage regarding doing well appear for students of arts-rich schools; in fact most categories show statistically significant differences for the arts-rich school participants. The advantages form a cluster that can be described as increased educational attainment and achievement.

Students attending arts-rich schools as opposed to arts-poor schools report more often that their postsecondary education experiences have led to better jobs and conditions associated with jobs (more pay, more responsibility, more promotion opportunity). The only indicator favoring the arts-poor students is a negative – they are about five times as likely to report dependence on public assistance at age 26.

***Doing Good* at age 26.** Indicators of *doing good* in the final NELS panel are displayed in figure 4.4 below. It can be seen readily that the balance of positive indications favoring students from arts-rich schools are related to academic success shown above and that there is a relative paucity of advantages in *doing good* for arts-rich school students. This becomes something of a theme in this chapter.

❋ ❋ ❋

Figure 4.4. Arts Rich vs. Arts Poor Schools
Indicators of contributions to community and society at age 26,
by attendance at arts rich versus arts poor high schools. Percentages by group.

	All Students		Low SES Students	
Doing Good	school type >		*Arts Rich*	*Arts Poor*
Youth organization volunteer	20.0		19.0	22.0
Civic/community volunteer	21.5	x	21.6	19.0
Participate in political campaign	3.6		1.5	3.8
Registered to vote	76.4		75.4	78.3
Voted in any election past 2 years	41.2	x	42.5	41.8
Voted in 1996 Presidential Election	55.0	x	53.7	51.4

(*) X = comparison favors arch rich schools, none statistically significant.

While the percentage figures tend to favor the arts-rich side of this ledger, none of the differences is significant.

Summing up: arts-rich versus arts-poor schools

This brief run-through our comparative assessment protocol shows that students attending schools we identified as arts-rich do better on some important outcomes, especially by the time they reach the age of 26. And even though all of our arts-rich students hail from the the lowest income group, they occasionally match the all-student population on important outcomes. In the anals of education research, it is hard to find average performance or outcome statistics reported for low-SES students that exceed such measures for the entire population. This would tend to indicate that the low-income group received some sort of advantage as they progressed on their goals – in fact, it would seem assured in this. The only difference in school experiences between arts-rich and arts-poor student experiences in our study was the one we measured for their schools – the richness versus paucity of their arts programs.

> *In the anals of education research, it is hard to find average performance or outcome statistics reported for low-SES students that exceed such measures for the entire population. This would tend to indicate that the low-income group received some sort of advantage as they progressed on their goals – in fact it would seem assured in this.*

Framing the *arts-rich* versus *arts-poor* school questions in another way.

The literature on arts-rich schools outlined above hints at an interesting possibility. A great deal of language in these reports discusses direct student participation in the visual and performing arts within arts-rich school communities. At the same time, another stream of thinking flows from these studies, a stream visible even in the brief presentation offered here. This is that arts-rich schools may have unique climates that bear on their effectiveness as well as on beliefs and dispositions within these school communities. *We hear of shared ethos, community of caring, shared ways of knowing, value for creativity in all of its forms, and outreach and integration with parents, community arts organizations, and to local citizens broadly.* These are strong words with potentially powerful implications. They are variously but commonly ascribed to arts-rich schools.

Of course, students in schools that scholars would call arts-rich, and also in the schools we have classified as arts-rich through our scaling methods, would be more likely to be what we in earlier chapters described as highly arts-engaged. Certainly more likely than students in our designated arts-poor schools.

But is the cluster of positive conditions reported to characterize arts-rich schools so influential that students within these schools are likely to benefit regardless of their orientations to or actual participation in the arts while enrolled? We might call this a halo effect for these schools. If evident, we might say to any child, arts-interested or not, get thee to an arts-infused or arts-rich school. Arts-rich schools are filled with determined teachers and kids, their curricula are coherent and integrated, their communities help out, and you'll have a better school experience.

This idea can be explored with the NELS data. This is because in fact, our arts-rich schools are not exclusively attended by high-arts students. There is a distribution favoring high-arts students of course – if only because the arts opportunities offered in arts-rich schools draw arts-interested students. But our arts-rich schools are attended by numbers of what we have called low-arts students – students who barely touch arts activities or classes.

We don't hear about this student in the literature – namely the student who goes through the arts-focused and arts-integrated high school who personally doesn't care much for the arts. Is such a school beneficial for this student? Does he or she really exist? Our guess is yes on the first, and NELS answers yes on the second question. Let's see how the NELS data inform these questions.

Methods. We replicate our previous routines to investigate the importance of arts-rich schools to students personally less inclined toward the arts. We consider this a modest test of overall climate and orientation in arts-rich schools that might benefit all students, the arts-inclined and others.

For this test we maintained our usual stance – we restricted our analysis to low-income students. Because the numbers of arts-disinterested students in arts-rich schools is fairly small, we faced two alternatives in setting up the analysis. If we used the low-income quartile of students and stuck to our restrictive definitions of arts-rich and arts-poor schools and high- and low-arts engagement, our sample of low-arts-engaged students enrolled in arts-rich schools would be too small to matter – about 40 students in all of NELS. We could relax our requirements in two principal ways. One would be to expand the definitions of arts-rich and arts-poor schools to increase the overall student numbers. Another would be to relax the family income requirement. As we worked out this problem, we were not satisfied with dramatically changing our arts-richness and engagement definitions, because these stand at the center of this query. We also did not want to use the entire NELS student population to test this either, because including high-SES students would obscure most of what we want to observe. So we compromised. We used the top third of schools on our arts-richness scale versus the bottom third, and students from the top third versus bottom third on our arts-engagement scale, and we used students from the low half of the family income spectrum only.

Thus we set up the analysis as: Do relatively low-arts-engaged students do better in arts-rich schools than in arts-poor schools. Our intention here is to explore effects of arts-rich schools on lower-income students who are not particularly attached to the arts per se: the halo effect of arts-richness.

Doing well and *doing good* at age 20.

In a consolidated format, we display *doing well* and *doing good* indicators in Figure 4.5 on the following page.

A brief scan of the figure suggests that at age 20, few differences emerge distinguishing the fortunes of non-arts-engaged students in arts-rich schools versus arts-poor school. But there are some differences. One is the advantage for arts-rich school students in enrolling in 4-year colleges after high school. Going back through our myriad comparisons for arts versus non-arts focus of various sorts, this difference is very common. The high-arts students compared with low-arts students, the high-arts students compared with high-sports students, students in arts-rich versus arts-poor school, and even students not much interested in art attending arts-rich versus arts-poor schools – all find their way more often to four-year colleges, by significant margins.

> *The high-arts students compared with low-arts students, the high-arts students compared with high-sports students, students in arts-rich versus arts-poor school, and even students not much interested in art attending arts-rich versus arts-poor schools — all find their way more often to four-year colleges, by significant margins.*

Two more familiar differences stand out here. One is that the students attending arts-rich schools are more likely to do some sort of performing arts after high school. In addition, these students are significantly more likely to involve themselves in religious activity. A nearly significant difference showing for the low-arts students attending arts-poor schools is that they are more likely to get involved in sports after high school. This makes sense. These students are not personally involved in art during school and they attend schools that offer comparatively little in the way of arts activities. Sports is a reasonable alternative interest for these students, one carrying forward beyond school.

James S. Catterall

Figure 4.5 Comparing Low-income, Low-art Student Outcomes in Arts-rich vs. Arts-poor High Schools at Age 20.

		N 12441	188	223
Doing Well -- Age 20		All students, all income levels	Arts Rich High Schools	Arts-Poor High schools
Sector for first college attended	2-year	29.3	30.3	33.6
	4-year	42.3	**40.4**	26.5 .
Doing What -- Age 20				
Does performing arts		7.5	6.9	3.6
Participates in sports		49.0	41.5	48.4
Participates in religious activities		39.6	**46.6**	33
3 or more hours of TV on weekdays		34.5	40	45.3
Doing Good -- Age 20			Arts Rich High Schools	Arts-Poor High schools
Volunteer work - any		27.9	26.1	35.0
Volunteered at hospitals		10.6	7.4	10.3
Volunteered, youth orgs, scouts		9.4	7.9	10.3
Vol. sports teams or sports clubs		6.4	4.3	3.6
Vol. church/related (not worship)		11.4	9.0	14.8
Vol. educational organizations		6.2	1.1	**4.5**
Vol. political clubs or organizations		3.1	2.7	3.6
Other volunteer work		7.1	3.7	6.3
Strong friendships very important		86.0	82.4	80.1

Focus here is on the performance of low-art students in arts-rich vs. art-poor high schools.
Bold figures indicate significant advantages for students one type of school vs. the other.
Bold differences are significant at p < .05 or better (Chi square, df2 >3.84).

Two indicators favoring low-arts students who attended arts-poor schools in this analysis are doing more volunteering more generally (which borders on statistical significance, and volunteering for educational organizations.

We turn next to age 26 and Figure 4.6 on the following page.

120

Figure 4.6 Comparing Low-income, Low-art Student Outcomes in Arts-rich vs. Arts-poor High Schools at Age 26.

	N	12441	188	223
Doing Well -- Age 26		*All Students*	*Arts Rich High Schools*	*Arts-Poor High schools*
Ever attended college after high school		79.1	80	84
Ever attended 4-yr post-sec. institution		53.8	**40.4**	26.5
Mostly As and Bs as undergraduate		31.0	**31.4**	20.2
Degree/certificate earned-2000	*MA+*	3.8	**3.2**	1.8
	BA+	29.6	**27.1**	17.3
	Assoc +	36.9	**43.7**	26.7
Holding full time job, 2000		75.3	75	71.3
Full time study, 2000		17.5	3.2	1.8
Dependence on public assistance				
Public aid in 1999		3.1	0.5	0.9
Public assistance-food stamps		2.3	1.1	2.2
Doing What -- Age 26				
Read papers or magazines 3+ days/wk.		67.8	98.9	94.1
Read any books		81	79.8	80.3
Ever go to public library		48.4	56.9	48.4
Ever attend plays, concerts		62.4	51.6	**69.0**
Participate in organized religion		56.2	69.0	65.5
Participate in sports		46.3	44.1	**64.0**
Doing Good -- Age 26				
Youth organization volunteer		20	20.2	20.2
Civic/community volunteer		21.5	23.4	20.6
Participate in political campaign		3.6	2.7	4.5
Registered to vote		76.4	76.1	78.9
Voted in any election, past 24 mos.		41.2	47.9	40.8
Voted, 1996 Presidential election (age 22)		55	59.0	52.9
Reflections on Own Education				
Education has led to better jobs		59.7	**61.2**	48.9
Education has led to higher pay		55.2	53.7	45.3
Education has led to more responsibility		60.0	**60.6**	50.7
Education leads to promotion opportunity		55.3	56.9	45.7
Aspire to BA+ by age 30		40.4	34.0	35.3

Focus here is on the shaded columns -- the the performance of low-art students in arts-rich versus art-poor high schools.

Bold figures indicate significant advantages for students involved in one group versus the other.
Bold differences are significant at p < .05 or better (Chi square, df2 >3.84).

121

Shown in Figure 4.6 are differences between low-arts students attending arts-rich versus arts-poor high schools. The figure is striking. All of the significant differences emerge in areas related to academic achievement and attainment. We saw a similar patterns when we assessed low-income students generally attending arts-rich as opposed to arts-poor high schools. Here as then, the students attending arts-rich high schools get further along in postsecondary education, get better grades, and feel more positively that their college experiences are impacting their jobs, terms of employment, and their future job prospects.

> *The low-arts students attending arts-rich high schools, when compared to those who attend arts-poor high schools, get further along in postsecondary education, get better grades, and feel more positively that their college experiences impact their jobs, terms of employment, and their future job prospects.*

As we concluded in our general analysis of the importance of arts-rich schools, few impacts on our *doing good* scales emerge. If there is an ethos, climate, compact, or other brand of cohesion binding the arts-rich schools in this study, it is a set of conditions that may accellerate academic progress. It almost certainly impacts the development of arts skills and sensitivities, something we cannot test through NELS. And we found no advantages captured in our citizenship or *doing good* measures.

How did our arts-rich and arts-poor schools differ?

In reflecting on where arts-rich and arts-poor schools seem to matter in this analysis, we went back to the NELS database to search for plausible effectiveness-related characteristics of schools to determine how the arts-rich and arts-poor schools in our sample differed. Based on what reported above, we might expect to find descriptors that could differentiate our arts-rich and arts-poor schools strictly on academic effectivess, as if the world were that simple. NELS is, after all, an *education* survey that does stress academic over other achievements among its indicators.

In Figure 4.7 we show the indicators we selected from NELS that might describe the sort of atmosphere of success the arts-rich school studies mention. It turns out that there are number of ways that these schools in fact differ, qualities suggesting comparatively positive conditions in the arts-rich schools.

When we scan our indicators, we would have to say that the arts-rich schools in our study differed from the arts-poor schools on many important dimensions. Teacher and student morale, teacher-student relations, and student behavior all favor the arts-rich school. And a host of instructional practices suggest that, at least at a meaningful margin, the teaching at arts-rich schools in geared toward deeper and more conceptual learning.

Figure 4.7

Comparative Qualities of Arts-rich and Arts-poor Schools
Reported by students and teachers

Percentages of <u>T</u>eachers/<u>S</u>tudents/<u>P</u>rincipals
Responding as indicated

Instructional practices	Arts Rich Schools	Arts Poor Schools	Who Reported:
Moderate to major emphasis on solving Problems in Math	80.0%	72.2%	T
Moderate to major emphasis on learnng facts and rules in Math	72.8%	74.0%	T
Small group instruction used 1 X week or more	30.1%	17.2%	T
Teachers lecture 2- x week or more	66.1%	76.9%	T
Students work from novels or plays 2-3 x per week or more	20.0%	7.0%	T
Students write impromptu essays 1 x week or more	10.6%	6.5%	T
Teachers have moderate to complete control of texts and materials	67.3%	55.6%	
Affective Quality of the School			
Teacher morale is low	6.7%	12.4%	A
Teachers partly or wholly agree with the statement: *"I am happy just to make it through the day."*	34.4%	51.5%	T
Student morale is high	36.1%	27.8%	A
Teacher Student Relations			
Teachers are interested in students	77.3%	73.2%	S
Students get along well with teachers	70.0%	66.9%	S
Student-Student Relations			
Students are friendly with other racial groups	81.7%	78.7%	S
Student racial conflict is rare or never	47.7%	43.8%	S
Student Behavior Indicators			
Tardiness is a serious problem	11.1%	17.8%	T
Students are rarely or never absent	45.0%	38.4%	A

T=teachers, A=administrators, S=students

The characteristics displayed in this figure have a unified quality. They point to practices in arts-rich schools that stand out in contemporary teaching and curriculum worlds as important conditions for effective schools. And the data also point to qualities of instruction that can produce deeper thinking about subjects and promote learning how to learn.

> *The qualities distinguishing arts-rich and arts-poor schools in NELS are stark, and we would expect these differences to show up in student achievement and development.*

> *Teacher and student morale, teacher-student relations, and student behavior all favor the arts-rich school. And a host of instructional practices suggest that, at least at a meaningful margin, the teaching at arts-rich schools aimed at deeper and more conceptual learning.*

First off, the indicators point to comparatively less emphasis in arts-rich schools on learning rules and facts and comparatively more emphasis on learning how to solve problems. Arts-rich schools do more collaborative learning – using almost twice as much small group instruction and significantly less teacher lecturing than the arts-poor schools. Students in arts-rich schools do much more work from novels and plays – three times as much as students in the arts-poor schools, and they do more impromptu writing. Teachers in arts-rich schools report more control over the texts and materials they use in their classes. The qualities distinguishing these two types of schools are stark and we would expect these differences to show up in student achievement and development.

> *Perhaps one so far un-mentioned comparison sums this up. About half of the teachers in arts-poor schools claim that they agree with the statement, "I am happy just to make it through the day." Things are better, but far from ideal, in the arts-rich schools, where only about of third of teachers agree with this statement.*

Chapter 5

English Language Learners (ELLs) in arts-rich versus arts-poor schools.

We turn here to a story within the arts-rich, arts-poor schools analysis. This is an exploration of the fortunes of English Language Learners in the NELS database. We do this not because it belongs here, or because it logically or necessarily falls at this point in our presentation. But because the opportunity lay before us and because we run across scant research in the arts that focuses on limited English speakers.

We have not seen NELS-based work on bilingual education, perhaps with some reason. This survey addresses high school, where limited English speaking student issues are different and less pervasive than in elementary schools. Also, the earliest administration of the NELS surveys, the 8th grade panel, was done in 1988, when issues of immigration, while significant, did not take on all of the complex dimensions and policy debates bearing on the topic in 2009.

There are two indicators in the 8th grade NELS survey that address student language issues. One is an indicator that the student herself speaks a language other than English. The second is an indicator that a language other than English is spoken in the student's home. It turns out that just about all students who responded yes to the second question (language other than English is spoken in the home) respond that they also spoke a language other than English.

Today, we use complex classification schemes to sort out how much written or spoken English students understand and can perform and whether this language is academic or colloquial, and use this information to prescribe a variety of instructional situations appropriate for individual children. NELS has no capacity for this type of sorting. We use the simple designation described above to identify a population reflecting this interest. Technically, ELL is not a correct label for the students we assign to this category – there is nothing to say that these youth were not perfectly competent speakers of English when they indicated their home language status, or that they could speak in another language. But, there is no doubt that limited English speakers populate our ELL classification in significant numbers. That's good enough for now.

We here track the same old question – how do ELL students fare in arts-rich high schools in comparison to arts-poor high school? For this analysis, we used both familiar and unfamiliar framing to run the numbers. On the familiar side, we used our traditional top-decile and bottom-decile definitions of arts-rich and arts-poor schools. Then because overall number of our ELLS in the database was small, and because this sub-population leaned heavily toward the low-income quartile, we used all ELL students as our population. So the question was simple – we wanted to compare the fortunes of all ELL students attending arts-rich schools with those attending arts-poor schools. We found 166 ELL students attending arts-rich schools and 160 attending arts-poor schools.

Figure 5.1 shows early indicators of *doing well* beyond high school for ELL students. As in our previous analyses, important academic progress differences stand out including attending a four-year college as a first postsecondary experience, and pursuing a BA degree at age 20. BA and higher-level degrees were expected by more ELLs attending arts-rich schools than arts-poor schools. These students also watch significantly less television. Many of the non-significant differences in Figure 5.1 favor the ELLs in arts-rich schools as well.

Figure 5.1 ENGLISH LANGUAGE LEARNERS IN ARTS RICH vs. ARTS POOR HIGH SCHOOLS

Education Attainments and Other Activities, Age 20.

Indicators of early postsecondary education and other activities at age 20, for low SES students, by attendance at arts rich versus arts poor high schools. Percentages by group.

		All Students		**ALL ELL STUDENTS**	
	N	12144		166	160
Doing Well		school type>>		*Arts Rich*	*Arts Poor*
Primarily a student in Jan 1994		85.1	X	90.2	81.7
Sector for first college attended	2-year	29.3		18.7	31.9
	4-year	42.3	X	**66.2**	43.3
Pursuing BA at age 20		35.6	X	**59.6**	39.4
Pursuing Associate degree		15.7		7.8	15.6
Involved in some post-sec. education		68.8	X	81.3	74.4
BA or higher expected		68.8	X	**88.6**	79.5
MA or higher expected		37.8	X	**62.9**	48.8
Doing What					
Does performing arts		7.5	X	**13.3**	7.5
2 or fewer hours of TV on weekdays		65.5	X	**77.7**	61.3
			(*)		

Bold figures indicate between-group percentage differences significant at p < .05 or better (N 166/160. Chi square, df2 >3.84).

(*) X = comparison favors arch rich schools, some not statistically significant.

✳ ✳ ✳

129

Doing good at age 20

Figure 5.2. ENGLISH LANGUAGE LEARNERS IN ARTS RICH vs.
ARTS POOR HIGH SCHOOLS

Community service activities at age 20,

		All Students		Low SES Students	
	N	12144		166	160
Doing Good		*school type>>*		*Arts Rich*	*Arts Poor*
Volunteer work - any		27.9	X	50.6	47.5
Volunteered at hospitals		10.6	X	**22.3**	10.0
Volunteered, youth orgs, scouts		9.4	X	15.7	11.3
Vol. sports teams or sports clubs		6.4		6.0	8.8
Vol. church/related (not worship)		11.4	X	16.9	15.8
Vol. educational organizations		6.2	X	10.2	8.1
Vol. political clubs or organizations		3.1		4.2	5.6
Other volunteer work		7.1		9	8.8
Strong friendships very important		92.4	X	86.1	81.9
Registered to vote, age 20		70.2	X	**71.7**	62.5
Voted in 1992 Presidential election		47.6	X	**48.8**	39.4
			(*)		

Bold figures indicate between-group percentage differences significant at p < .05 or better (N 166/160. Chi square, df2 >3.84).

(*) X = comparison favors arch rich schools, some not statistically significant.

Figure 5.2 captures our indicators of service and community at age 20. Because the samples are small, even the nearly 10 percent differences in the two voting behavior indicators are not significantly different by statistical conventions. Most of the indicators here do favor the students attending arts-rich schools (marked with an X). Volunteering at hospitals is more common among arts-rich high school graduates than arts-poor graduates. With these small samples, and with an array of volunteer behavior indicators showing small to medium differences favoring the arts-rich school students, it is reasonable to say that this group in fact reports more voluntarism than ELLs from the arts-poor schools.

Doing well at age 26.

Figure 5.3 displays indicators of *doing well* at age 26 for ELL students in arts-rich versus arts-poor schools. The profile is familiar to those shown in other arts-rich versus arts-poor

---

Figure 5.3. ENGLISH LANGUAGE LEARNERS IN ARTS RICH vs. ARTS POOR HIGH SCHOOLS

Indicators of higher education and employment-related attainment at age 26, by attendance at arts rich versus arts poor high schools. Percentages by group.

		All Students		Low SES Students	
	N	12144		166	160
A. Doing Well		school type>>		Arts Rich	Arts Poor
Ever attended college after high school		79.1	X	92.8	87.5
Ever attended 4 year college		53.8	X	**77.7**	58.1
Mostly As and Bs as undergraduate		31.0	X	34.9	29.4
Degrees earned as of age 26	MA+	3.8	X	**9**	3.8
	BA+	29.6	X	**58.4**	33.1
	AA+	36.9	X	**61.4**	45.7
Holding full time job as of 2000		75.3		65.1	65.6
Attending academic institution, 2000		17.5	X	10.2	5.6
education has led to better jobs		59.7		**78.3**	63.7
education has led to higher pay		55.2	X	**74.1**	58.1
education has led to more responsibility		60.0	X	**77.1**	66.9
education leads to promotion opportunity		55.3	X	**76.5**	59.4
Read any books		81	X	88.0	80.6
Ever go to public library		48.4		50.6	54.4
Ever attend plays, concerts		62.4		65.0	70.6
Ever participate in sports		53.7		48.2	48.8

Bold figures indicate between-group percentage differences significant at p < .05 or better (N 166/160. Chi square, df2 >3.84).

(*) X = comparison favors arch rich schools, some not statistically significant.

---

school comparisons. ELL students from arts-rich schools attend four-year colleges more frequently and are much more likely to have earned a BA degree by age 26 (58 percent versus 33 percent).

ELL students in arts-rich schools also believe that their postsecondary education has benefited them through securing better jobs, higher pay, more responsibility, and more promotion opportunity. It is interesting to note that the ELL students from arts-rich schools frequently outscore the average student in NELS on our measures of *doing well*, as do the ELL students in arts-poor high schools on a few indicators. For example, 58 percent of the arts-rich students earned BA degrees by age 26, surpassing the 33 percent of ELL students from arts-poor schools. But even the arts-poor ELL group did better on this measure than the average student, based on all 12,000 NELS students where only about 30 percent had earned BAs by the same age.

> *It is interesting to note that the ELL students from arts-rich schools frequently outscore the average student in NELS, as do the ELL students in arts-poor high schools on a few indicators. For example, 58 percent of the arts-rich ELL students earned BA degrees by age 26, surpassing the 33 percent of ELL students from arts-poor schools as well as the 30 percent average BA attainment level for all 12,000 students in the NELS database.*

Doing Good at Age 26

There are no significant differences to report between students attending arts-rich and arts-poor schools in the *doing good* measures shown in Figure 5.4. The difference shown in the Presidential vote is sizeable, 60 percent versus 52 percent. But given the sample size, this difference could have resulted from random error. About half of the indicators favor students from the arts-rich schools.

Figure 5.4. ENGLISH LANGUAGE LEARNERS IN ARTS RICH vs. ARTS POOR HIGH SCHOOLS

Indicators of contributions to community and society at age 26,
by attendance at arts rich versus arts poor high schools. Percentages by group.

Doing Good	All Students school type >		Low SES Students Arts Rich	Arts Poor
Youth organization volunteer	20.0		22.9	26.3
Civic/community volunteer	21.5	X	28.3	22.5
Participate in political campaign	3.6		4.2	5.6
Registered to vote	76.4		74.7	74.4
Voted in any election past 2 years	41.2	X	41.6	37.5
Voted in 1996 Presidential Election	55.0	X	60.2	51.9

(*) X = comparison favors arch rich schools, none statistically significant.

A cluster of related differences characterize our comparisons of arts-rich versus arts-poor schools in all three of our analyses, including our assessment targeting ELL students. This is that the arts-rich school students progress in their education after high school more quickly, they earn more degrees by age 26, and they feel more positively that their postsecondary education experiences have benefited them in the world of work.

In all of our analyses, including outcomes for ELL students here in Chapter 5, students who attended arts-rich schools progress in formal education after high school more quickly, they earn more degrees by age 26, and they feel more positively that their postsecondary education experiences have benefited them in the world of work.

Chapter 6
Reflective Learning, the Autonomous Brain,
and the Case for Effect

Conscious inner and social conversation, unconscious brain
restructuring, and transfer.

Introduction.

This chapter presents two central arguments supporting our
contentions in earlier chapters that high level involvement and
learning in the arts in secondary school leads to increased
performance and enhanced social values in later years. Most
research related to this topic, as well as to learning more
generally, is based on studies that last a matter of minutes,
hours, days, weeks, or sometimes months. For example, the
earliest "Mozart effect" studies were based on 20 minutes of
music listening by college students. The researchers measured
spatial reasoning effects immediately after the listening
experience and again a few weeks later. Studies lasting
longer, such as the assessment of Whirlwind's movement
program, examined a school year of dance and movement
lessons followed by tests of literacy.[xxxviii] An extreme case of
scholarly persistence is the six-year evaluation of the Chicago
Arts Partnerships in Education, where student tests scores in
language and mathematics were monitored throughout and
where end-of-program debriefings of students, teachers, and
school administrators were conducted over two years.[xxxix]

A principal virtue of the analyses reported in this book is their
focus on the status and activities of study participants long
after the arts experiences of interest. Our research addresses
gradual and cumulative developments that researchers often
project as possible from short-term research findings. The
same researchers seldom return to check 12 years later. Here
we have 12,000 subjects whose experiences are extensively
documented and reported more 8 to 12 years after the
subjects' secondary school arts experiences.

In this final chapter, we'd like to return to debates about why engagement and learning in the arts could lead to the outcomes we pursued in this research. We ground this discussion on review we presented in the inaugural issue of the *Journal of Learning in the Arts* in 2005, copies of which are in the hands of about 3000 downloading readers.[xl] This review likens processes that transfer knowledge from one domain to another as coming from interactions that we call inner and outer conversations, and from autonomous developments in the brain we capture with the term "silence."

Conversation and silence. By "conversation and silence" we signal two critical ways that children learn through the arts, among other metaphors for processes of learning. *Conversation* refers to both inner as well as interpersonal dialogues involved in the creative and expressive processes common to all arts disciplines. The inner conversation of artistic creation is a metacognitive activity in which the artist "steps back" to consider thoughts and thinking processes. (Bruner, 1960; Bruner, 1966). The interpersonal conversation can prompt creative reflection through a process that could be called *assisted* metacognition. *Silence* in this discussion refers to subconscious brain function and cognitive re-structuring – the neurological bridge that may link learning in the arts on the one hand with non-arts related understandings and skills on the other hand. At least by inference, both mechanisms of learning through the arts receive attention and support in the research literature.[xli] We stress these two sorts of mechanisms in considering the academic and socio-emotional developments presented in this book.

Conversations and Learning Through Art

Although "conversation" has not been established as the principal cognitive dynamic bearing on learning through the arts, we want to focus on two sorts of conversation or dialogue as fundamental ways that children can learn while forming and considering their creative expressions and while collaborating and performing in the arts. Conversation is both a real and metaphorical perspective on individual and socially mediated learning. The conversations of interest are both the social exchanges and verbalized reflections surrounding art (the real) and also the conversations within the individual art-creator as his or her work takes form (the inner, *as if* conversation).[xlii] These conversations are readily seen in the context of theories of knowledge acquisition more generally. Vigotsky (1978), Lave (1988) and others point to the essentially social nature of learning, which the idea of the learning conversation surely reflects. The inner conversation is metacognitive in nature, involving coming to understand by reflecting on one's thinking and thinking processes (Bruner, 1960; 1966).

Arts-focused learning conversation appears to be a useful conception for unpacking learning through the arts; but its scholarly documentation is thin. Researchers know artistic activity when they see it, recognize a finished product placed before them, and sometimes measure learning appearing to have occurred by the end of the process. But the intervening conversations are not formally mapped. Certainly a critical feature of learning through conversation is that dialogic processes can be fruitfully manipulated, both by the creators themselves as they work, and also by art specialists, classroom teachers, and parents who can help guide conversations in ways that promote learning. This scaffolding of the learning experience is recognized as beneficial if not critically important in research on teaching and learning. It's a topic that bears on the discussion that follows and one to which we return when we explore implications.[xliii]

Social Conversation and Learning

Social conversation refers to verbal interaction between an artist and observers of an artwork, or simply between or among individuals beholding a work of art. A timeless example of the instructional potential of social conversation involving art is the use of period art prints in social studies and history textbooks, or museum visits, or in post discussions of musical, theatrical, or dance performances. Consider a case in point. Reflective questioning as well as interpersonal dialogue spawned by Picasso's *Guernica* may be expected to promote understandings, insights, conjectures, and potential measures about the painting and its various contexts. Since the artist himself has neither said nor written much about this painting as far as the public record goes, the masterpiece is fertile ground for making meaning out of images and symbols. To some, the game is, "What did Picasso mean by this, or symbolize by that?" But the real fun may be in the interactive processes linking painting and observer, or among observers examining the work. Apart from the obvious "big" interpretations of *Guernica* heralded in textbooks and art volumes, just whether or not Picasso meant particular things is only a touchstone to learning through the painting. It can be instructive for children to draw their own inferences from the work and place them in the context of contemporary social or political issues.

It is natural to see in *Guernica* a depiction of horrible events occurring during the Spanish Civil War. But much more is suggested, for one example its foreshadowing of Hitler's rise on the continent. Here *Guernica* conveys a stark message about the future of war and the imminent fate of Europe. At the very least, *Guernica* depicts the cruelty and the near hopelessness of war. It is an extraordinarily complex picture. It can be examined artistically and sociologically, as well as politically – just to warm up. Its finished form and preliminary sketches could support an entire unit of historical study. But to attain rich learning through this or any work of art, or through observing or participating in any work in the visual or performing arts, children generally need to reflect, discuss, and reflect again.

Such is the learning conversation – conversations that also stand to benefit from more expert others to pave the way. Works of art may be variously inspiring in their own right to children of diverse dispositions, but some organization and leadership in approaching works of art in the name of learning seem essential. Mindful staring is a great beginning. Looking up the painting in a library (or on the Internet) and reading critical commentary is a good way to progress. Asking children individually or in groups to identify symbols within the painting and to articulate or write about their meanings is another. General discussions of how symbols function and what makes for an effective symbol are others. And asking children to write about an issue or issues involved with *Guernica* using literary metaphor and symbolism might cap a series of lessons. [xliv]

All of this can be rich, hands-on, interactive, and inspiring work. It is an instructive model for learning through visual art and by analogy through all art forms. However, it signals a set of explorations that have little likelihood of occurring without the guidance of a knowledgeable teacher or mentor, the art or general classroom teacher who knows enough about both history and art to connect works of art to a moment in history or to an age in science or literature. And devoutly to be wished is the teacher who knows the value of giving kids the freedom to assert and defend their own opinions without the burden of having to come up with an arbitrary and elusive single right answer. Absent these dispositions, we can hope for the teacher motivated to learn in these respects. [xlv]

The inner conversation and learning

Producing a work of art engages the artist in a personal iterative exploration of ideas and emotions as the work proceeds. We call this the inner conversation of the creative process. [xlvi] Painting, playwriting, choreographing, composing, or any artistic creation can engage the artist in drawing on and deepening knowledge related to the artistic form--as examples, human anatomy, motivations and behavior, history, and the built environment. Intensive study and response to artwork by both artists and non-artists can elicit similar processes in the respondent; in this way the arts present a learning experience for both artist and audience.

Advances in the theories and methods of the cognitive sciences (and in the neurosciences discussed presently) make possible new explorations of these prospects for the arts and their importance for human education and development. Each of the art forms engages in particular ways specific physical, cognitive, and affective processes. And the conversations we refer to are by no means restricted to the creation and exploration of visual art. They apply equally to performance and creation in music, dance, and theatre. Outer and inner conversations abound in any learning setting, with or without external facilitation.

Exploring the expressive activities of drawing, sculpting, composing, dramatizing, choreographing, or writing poetry might add to the understanding of the cognitive processes engaged in learning and could yield insights important to the quest for effective educational practices. Opportunities to experience the iterative processes of "art making," or inner conversations (continually refining ideas based on formative self-assessment) may be especially valuable for enhancing students' abilities to learn both within and beyond the arts.

An example of inner conversation that most academic readers will recognize is the learning spawned by the writing process itself, where things are seen anew through the processes of writing, reviewing, and revising as well as through processes of re-considering and re-conceptualizing. In addition and perhaps just as important, attempts to create a story or narrative commensurate to the expressive goals may engender learning of a different sort. This is growth in the understanding of relationships among the ideas important to the story and thus important to a full understanding of the theme or topic at hand. In the end, efforts to write almost universally prompt authors to say that they learned about their subject through the very act of writing. This process bears the hallmarks of the inner conversation. Yet we who seek scholarly understandings of artistic creation seldom listen in on the creators, at least not systematically.

Silence – brain at work

By *silence*, or subconscious transfer, we refer to neuro-dynamic learning processes that take place without awareness on the part of the learner. The most heralded example of this invisible activity pertaining to the arts is research that investigates learning in music and the consequential enhancement of spatial reasoning or other abilities. The 9 year-old piano student works with no awareness that she might over time be gaining facility for fractions and proportions in her math lessons.[xlvii] *Silence* more specifically refers to the neuro-function of involvement and learning in art and hypothesized processes of transfer from this learning. Research suggests that learning in art, and particularly in certain kinds of music, brings change to neural pathways and neuronal firing patterns. The Rosetta stone for understanding transfer from learning in the arts to other domains may emerge as *comprehension of the impact of arts-related neurological development on individual abilities to accomplish non-arts tasks*.

This is an area of research that is proving to be a magnet for cognitive neuroscientists and learning psychologists, as well as for education philanthropists. This work is tremendously exciting as well. It brings a novel scientific discipline to the study of art and promotes a fertile laboratory for exploring brain-function correlates of cognition and emotion.[xlviii]

Neuroscience evidence to date should be characterized first as expanding understanding of the "human brain on art." This sort of advance comes through imaging brain function while a subject learns, performs, or experiences art. A second characterization stems from hypotheses building in the complex area of the neuro-function of learning and resulting skill transfer. Even the most developed areas of research in the arts and cognition do not reach much beyond these boundaries. Consider as evidence the fact that significant growth in sustained spatial reasoning ability and its consequential effects on performance in mathematics remains supported by only a small number of studies. Published brain imaging studies do not map such relationships. Traditions in science hold that one comprehends human phenomena only through an accumulation of studies, and not through any single piece of research. Thus, music and spatial reasoning research, while intuitively satisfying and widely touted, is in a fairly early stage of development.

Our abilities to discern, measure, and decode neural function at different levels of structure and degrees of resolution make linking neuro-function and learning in and through the arts most promising. Our understandings of the dynamics of brain chemistry grow apace. Important investigations unable to be done today will surely become feasible in a matter of very few years.

Returning to theory. This is a good point in the discussion to remind ourselves of the primary theoretical foundations of "silent" transfer of learning: i.e. change in knowledge, skills, dispositions, and orientations stemming from neural processes stimulated by learning in or participation in the arts. The central theory has two main points:

- Arts learning and experiences, to varying degrees, reorganize neural pathways, or the way the brain functions. Extended and or deep learning in the arts reinforces these developments.

- The development and re-organization of brain function due to learning in the arts *may* impact how and how well the brain processes other tasks.

This is the essential conception of transfer at the neuronal level. The crucial questions arising from the theory are:

- Which neuro-functions are impacted by learning in specific art forms?

- To what degree are these functions affected?

- What are the implications of such changes for skill or motivational developments in non-artistic domains?

- Do such skill developments matter? Are the changes of any significance?) And,

- Do measured changes last? Or are they fleeting in character?

Surely the piano-learning example discussed briefly above engages these questions, even if alteration of neural pathways is not a full description or metaphor for the changes in the brain necessary to facilitate transfer. And many educators will notice the parallels between this fundamental theory of transfer and today's established theories of constructivist learning (dating to the works of Jerome Bruner).[xlix] These convictions hold that learning is rooted in interactions between new information and emotions on the one hand, and existing cognitive structures on the other hand. The results of such interactions are new cognitive structures.

Summing up. This chapter presents a brief sketch of two models of learning in the visual and performing arts with implications for the transfer of learning. One model is based on the potential fruits of conversations engaged in by the artist as a work of art unfolds. Examples included learning something by writing about it and engaging great works of art to learn history, such as Picasso's *Guernica*. Conversations speculate about meaning, debate symbol systems, and help make connections. Such conversations take place both within the individual and also between and among individuals. They apply to music, dance, theatre, and visual art with equanimity. Artists young and old have inner conversations; the worlds of the visual and performing arts are hotbeds of student and student-adult interactions – where live conversations reign.

The second model of transfer is based on the inevitability of autonomous cognitive change through engagement in art and the possible implications of such change on non-arts skills, capacities, and emotions. Cognitive re-structuring is sometimes discerned through neuro-imaging, but changes in brain function remain both mysterious and silent. The vital question emerging from this brain-based conception of transfer is not whether brains rewire themselves through arts experiences. They inevitably will do so, if only to an untraceable degree. The critical questions are rather whether or not, where, and how any such arts-inspired "re-wirings" impact brain processes that help with non-arts tasks. That is, can we draw accurate inferences about transfer of learning through the arts from brain images or from measures of brain activity?

The important implications of this discussion are its suggestions for the conversations embedded in art learning, art making, art performance, and art appreciation. The discussion speaks also to future inquiry. It is not about the practical consequences of transfer of learning through the arts that may be supported by research and not about individual decisions concerning when to initiate piano lessons. The implications point to what we suspect, but in most respects don't know, about the mechanisms of creative work and the processes of learning through creative expression. Whether we speak of brain function or the learning conversations of children, we know very little about what goes on in the mind while creating or confronting art. If the conversations discussed here are important for how children create and what they learn from creating, we need to know more about these conversations. The interactions of children around art should be a focus of research; so should the reflective processes of the young artist as a work goes from the spark of an idea to finished product, from block of clay to sculpture, or from children's story to dramatized play or dance. The individual is at the center of the creative process, and how young minds create in the worlds of art and beyond is worth up-close and continuing study.

A further implication is the suggestion of the potential benefits of understanding the role that others, typically teachers, can play in catalyzing or otherwise inspiring, reflective conversations. Vygotsky would place this practice within a structure he calls scaffolding.[1] If the learning conversation is important, it would behoove the attentive teacher, peer, or parent to nudge, beckon, guide, model, and otherwise spark learning conversations. Understandings of the conversation process may point others in directions boosting their helpfulness.

No one needs convincing that the marriage of art and neuroscience has enticing potential; yet it is still engaged in a lengthy honeymoon. If art is about thinking, and thinking is about how the brain works, we should expect exponential growth over the coming years in our comprehension of the neuro-physiology of thinking and emotion, as well as about how the arts interact with more general capacities of the brain.

Does this inform the research we reported in previous chapters?

We cannot firmly affix the theoretical nets of conversation or neuro-function to the phenomena we illuminated in earlier chapters, but we identify these mechanisms as likely co-conspirators in the positive associations we reported. That is if learning through doing art spills over to valued human capacities, this probably takes place in part through social interactions and metacognitive processes sparked by the arts experience. Transfer probably also occurs through changes in the brain, through neural pathways redirected and reinforced by intensive work in the arts over long periods of time as a youth. Or by long-term immersion in arts-rich school cultures that have a feel, patterns of human connections, common beliefs about children and youth, coherent ideas about learning, and an overall cohesive quality that frees up and encourages all of the parts to work together.

> *If learning through doing art spills over to valued human capacities, this probably takes place in part through social interactions and metacognitive processes sparked by the arts experience. Transfer also occurs through redirecting neural pathways through intense experience. That such events are more likely for highly arts engaged students than for arts-poor students seems reasonable.*

Among other requirements, it would take great resolution in observations of individuals in their high arts-involved states, or high athletics-involved states, to confirm these hypotheses. The same can be said for our understandings of arts-rich and arts-poor schools and the implications of these differences for the academic and social development of youth.

Our work leads us to believe that individual artistic engagement can spark long-term positive developments for students, and that cohesive arts-rich cultures in schools also produce outcomes we have called *doing well,* and *doing good by doing art.*

INDEX

Endnotes

[i] This chapter is based on a 1999 report of our analysis of the NELS:88 arts involvement data between 8th and 12th grades. This report was published as Involvement in the Arts and Human Development: General Involvement and Intensive Involvement In Music and Theatre Arts by James S. Catterall, Richard Chapleau, and John Iwanaga. Chapter in Edward B. Fiske (Ed.), <u>Champions of Change: The Impact of the Arts on Learning</u>. Washington DC: The Arts Education Partnership; The President's Committee on the Arts and Humanities; The John D. and Catherine T. MacArthur Foundation; and the GE Fund.

[ii] NELS:88 is managed by the Institute of Education Sciences/National Center for Education Statistics at the United States Department of Education. The data and codebooks are available in various forms on CD Rom media for public use.

[iii] Socioeconomic status is a measure of parent education level, income, and type of job(s) held by parents.

[iv] Catterall, J. S. <u>Involvement in the Arts and Success in Secondary School</u>. Washington DC: Americans for the Arts. Monograph Series V. 1, No. 9, January 1998.

[v] See Darby, J. T. and Catterall, J. S. The fourth R: The arts and learning. *Teachers College Record*, <u>96</u>(2), 1994.

[vi] See Gardner, H.: *Frames of Mind* (New York: Basic Books), 1983; and *The Arts and Human Development* (New York: John Wiley), 1973.

[vii] See Morrison Institute of Public Policy and The National Endowment for the Arts: *Schools, Communities, and the Arts: A Research Compendium*. Tempe, AZ: The Morrison Institute for Public Policy, Arizona State University and the National Endowment for the Arts (1995). Especially summary of the report on the National Longitudinal Study of *Different Ways of Knowing* (The Galef Institute, Los Angeles). See also Catterall, J.S. "The Chicago Arts Partnerships in Education: Summary Evaluation." With Lynn A. Waldorf. Chapter in Edward B. Fiske (Ed.), *Champions of Change: The Impact of the Arts on Learning*. The Arts Education Partnership; The President's Committee on the Arts and Humanities;

The John D. and Catherine T. MacArthur Foundation; and the GE Fund. 1999. (47-62)

[viii] See Catterall, J.S. and Peppler, K.A. (2007). "Learning in the visual arts and the worldviews of young children." *Cambridge (UK) Journal of Education.* 37:4, 543 - 560

[ix] Coleman, J. (1961). *The Adolescent Society.* Westbrook CT: Greenwood Press. Coleman, J.(1966) *Equality of Educational Opportunity Study.* Washington, DC: U.S. Department of Health, Education, and Welfare, Office of Education. Catterall, J. S. Standards and school dropouts: A national study of tests required for high school graduation." *American Journal of Education, 98(1),* November 1989, 1-34.

[x] A note on our methods for scaling outcome differences between groups is contained in Chapter 2.

[xi] *Critical Links: Learning in the Arts and Student Academic and Social Development.* Washington DC: National Endowment for the Arts, The Arts Education Partnership. (with Richard Deasy (Ed.) and others, 2002. Special issue of *The Journal of Aesthetic Education: The Arts and Academic Achievement; What the Evidence Shows* University of Illinois Press,Volume 34, nos. 3/4, Fall/Winter, 2000.

[xii] Rauscher, F.H., & Zupan, M.A.(2000). Classroom keyboard instruction improves kindergarten children's spatial-temporal performance: A field experiment. *Early Childhood Research Quarterly, 15,* 215-228.

[xiii] Bahna-James (1991). Schllenberg, G. (2004). Catterall. & Rauscher (2007). *Unpacking the effects of music on intelligence.* Chapter in F. Rauscher, W. Gruhn (Ed.) Neurosciences in Music Pedagogy. Hauppauge NY: Nova Science Publishers, (2007).

[xiv] See Coward, 1990, for a general presentation on pattern thinking with applications to the game of chess. For extensions to music and cognition, see: Boettcher, Hahn & Shaw, 1994; Grandin, Peterson & Shaw, 1998; Graziano, Shaw & Wright, 1997; Rauscher & Shaw, 1997, and Rauscher & Shaw, 1998.

[xv] See Jackson, T, Learning Through Theatre: new perspectives on theatre in education. Second edition. London: Routledge, 1993.

[xvi] See Bolton, G. *Drama as Education: an argument for placing drama at the center of the curriculum.* London: Longman, 1984.

[xvii] Jackson, op. cit, p. 44.

[xviii] Johnson & O'Neill (1984), p. 129.

[xix] Jackson, T. (1980). Learning Through Theatre: Essays and Casebooks on Theatre in Education. Manchester: Manchester University, 1980. Also Dorothy Heathcote, *Drama and Learning,* Chapter in Johnson & O'Neill, (1984) pp. 90-102.

[xx] See Chapter in E. Fiske (Ed.), 1999, 47-62. The sixth-year evaluation of the Chicago Arts Partnerships in Education. This chapter presents discussions and evidence concerning integration of the arts into the academic curriculum.

[xxi] Lindblom and Cohen make this argument for much of social science in their classic book. Lindblom, C. E. and Cohen, D. K. (1979). *Usable Knowledge: Social Science and Social Problem Solving.* New Haven, CT: Yale University Press.

[xxii] The Imagination Project conducted such an investigation – the 6th year evaluation of the Chicago Arts Partnerships in Education referenced in endnote 20 and elsewhere.

[xxiii] See Catterall, J.S. (1998). "Risk and Resilience in Student Transitions to High School." *American Journal of Education* 106/2 (February, 1998), 302-333.

[xxiv] The Wisc III (Wechsler) test of intelligence, the most frequently used and cited test of intelligence for young children, partitions its assessment tasks into two domains labeled Verbal and Performance Scales. Music learning associates more with the Performance Scale of the Wisc III intelligence battery than with its Verbal Scale. (Catterall & Rauscher, 2007).

[xxv] Catterall, J. S. "Standards and School Dropouts: A National Study of Tests Required for High School Graduation." *American Journal of Education, 98(1),* November 1989, 1-34.

[xxvi] We note that our measures of statistical significance of group differences depend on the measured (and displayed) size of group differences as well as on the sizes of the groups in

question. These measures, like all determinations of statistically significant difference, take into account measurement error arising from various sources. Extreme systematic bias in reporting on a variable would tend to exaggerate measured group differences and lead to overestimates of their statistical significance.

[xxvii] A note on percentage differences. If one group shows 15 percent of its members participating in an activity and another group shows 10 percent participating, this is typically described in one of two ways, depending on the context of explanation. One approach is to say that there is a 5-percentage point difference between the two groups. It is this difference that is subjected to the Chi Square statistical tests of significance. Another approach is to claim that the first group's participation in this activity is 50 percent higher than the second group's participation – because 15 percent is 1.5 times the magnitude of 10 percent, and thus 50 percent greater.

[xxviii] Fiske, E. (Ed.) (1999). *Champions of Change.* op. cit.

[xxix] Schellenberg, E.G. (2004). Music lessons enhance IQ. *Psychological Science, 15,* 511 514. Also Catterall, J. S. and Rauscher, F. "Unpacking the impact of music on intelligence." (With Frances Rauscher). Chapter in *Neurosciences and Music Pedagogy.* W. Gruhn (Ed.). Hauppage, NY: Nova Science Publishers (2007).

[xxx] See Arts Education Partnership (2006), Noblit, et al. A+ Schools Evaluation (Program Report), Horowitz & Webb-Dempsey (2002), *Multi-arts Programs.* Chapter in Deasy (2002).

[xxxi] Fiske, E. (ed.) Champions of Change op. cit.

[xxxii] Catterall, J. S. (1998). *Risk and resilience in student transitions to high school.* op.cit.

[xxxiii] See for example various works of Robert Pace on the value of involvement on campus and success in higher education.

[xxxiv] The 2008 report of Douglas Hartmann to the LA84 Foundation presents such a review.

[xxxv] This characterization of Eccles's work comes from the (2005) Fisher & Lerner Encyclopedia of Developmental Science, p. 857.

xxxvi Stevenson, L. M. and Deasy, R.J. (2005). *Third Space: When Learning Matters.* Washington DC: Arts Education Partnership.

xxxvii Noblit et al. (2000) The A+ Schools Evaluation. op. cit.

xxxviii The Whirlwind study is reported in Critical Links, pp. 36-37.

xxxix Catterall, J. (1999). CAPE evaluation, op. cit.

xl Catterall, J. S. (2005). Conversation and silence: Transfer of learning from the arts. *Journal of Learning through the Arts*, 1, 1, 1-13.

xli Reviewers of previous drafts have pointed to the unquestioned parallels between the learning conversation described here and both dialogic inquiry and dialectic processes.

xlii Other contributors to the inaugural issue of the *Journal of Learning Through the Arts* (V 1,1, 2005) offer views of the creative process that at least implicitly point to processes of inner and social conversation in the sense described here. Peterson (2006) works with the interpersonal or social construction of cognition. She also points to the neurological organization of cognitive development in ways complementing the discussion of *silence* in this article. Brouillette & Burns (2006) suggest that both inner and social conversations impact artists who become teaching artists – experiences that fold back to impact their own work as artists. And two articles discuss the creation and manipulation of visual images in reflective, metacognitive manners. Foley (2006) describes individuals integrating their own visual imagery with imagery from other cultures as a reflective process of cultural learning. In a like-minded study, Beck, Cummins, &Yep (2006) explore rendering abstract ideas, e.g. *peace*, through photographic imagery in three different cultures. Like the photographer exposing five rolls of film in order to get something right, one envisions the artists in this study conversing with their proof sheets to explore and converge on the right images.

xliii See: Berk, L. E. & Winsler, A. (1995). Scaffolding Children's Learning: Vigotsky and Early Childhood Education. National Association for the Young Children.

Washington, DC. Published in: School Psychology International. (1998). Vol. 19, #2, pp. 189-191.

[xliv] Both David Perkins of Project Zero and Kevin McCarthy of the Rand Corporation probe learning involved in viewing works of art. Perkins, D. (1994). *The Intelligent Eye: Learning to Think by Looking at Art*. Los Angeles: The Getty Trust. Also, McCarthy, K. et al. (2005). *Gifts of the muse: Reframing the Debate about the Benefits of the Arts*. Santa Monica: The Rand Corporation, a project supported by the Wallace Foundation.

[xlv] See Gordon Wells, Ed. (1999). *Dialogic Inquiry Towards a Socio-cultural Practice and Theory of Education*.

[xlvi] This section draws on an entry in the volume, "The Arts and Education: New Opportunities for Research." Washington DC: Arts Education Partnership, p. 7, 2004. Richard Deasy, Paul Goren, Steve Seidel and James Catterall participated in writing this and other cognition-related sections of the book.

[xlvii] The AEP agenda cited *op cit.* contributes a brief discussion of such dialogues as a process worthy of future research. (p. 7)

[xlviii] An illustration of new directions in research on learning in the arts is *Arts and Cognition: Progress Report on Brain Research*. New York: Dana Foundation and the Dana Alliance for Brain Initiatives (2005). Especially the featured essay by Michael S Gazzaniga, Ph.D.

[xlix] Bruner (1960; 1966). (See References and Resources.)

[l] See NAYC: *Scaffolding Children's Learning: Vygotsky and Early Childhood Education*. National Association for the Young Children. Washington, DC, 1995.

References and Resources

Transfer of Learning from the Arts

Berk, L. E. and Winsler, A. (1998). Scaffolding Children's Learning: Vygotsky and Early Childhood Education. *School Psychology International,* 19/2 pp. 189-191.

Beck, R. J., Cummins, J., and Yep, J., (2006). Picturing Peace: Local and Universal Symbols in Three Cultures. This issue.

Brouillette, L. and Burns, M. (2006). ArtsBridge America: Bringing the Arts Back to School. This issue.

Deasy, R. (Ed.) (2004). "The Arts and Education: New Opportunities for Research." Washington DC: Arts Education Partnership.

Dana Foundation (2005). *Arts and Cognition: Progress Report on Brain Research.* New York: Dana Foundation and the Dana Alliance for Brain Initiatives.

Foley, K. (2006). Wayang and Gamelan as a Tool of Cultural Learning: Indonesian Puppets, Dance and Music in the Classroom. This issue.

Lave, J. (1988) *Cognition in Practice: Mind, Mathematics, and Culture in Everyday Life.* Cambridge, UK: Cambridge University Press.

McCarthy, K. et al. (2005). *Gifts of the muse: Reframing the Debate about the Benefits of the Arts.* Santa Monica: The Rand Corporation.

NAYC (1995). *Scaffolding Children's Learning: Vygotsky and Early Childhood Education.* Washington, DC: National Association for the Young Children.

Perkins, D. (1994), *The Intelligent Eye: Learning to Think by Looking at Art.* Los Angeles: The Getty Trust.

Peterson, R. (2006). Crossing Bridges That Connect the Arts, Cognitive Development and the Brain. Journal of Learning Through the Arts (2005).

Vygotsky, L. (1978). *Mind in Society.* Cambridge, MA: Harvard University Press.

Wells, G. (Ed.). (1999). *Dialogic Inquiry Towards a Socio-cultural Practice and Theory of Education.* Cambridge, UK: Cambridge University Press.

Winner, E. and Hetland, L. (2006) Cognitive transfer from arts education to non-arts outcomes: Research evidence and policy outcomes, in: E. Eisner and M. Day (Eds.) *Handbook on Research and Policy in Art Education* (National Art Education Association).

Arts, Efficacy, and Agency

Bandura, A. (1986) Social foundations of thought and action: A social cognitive perspective (Englewood Cliffs, New Jersey, Prentice Hall).

Bransford, J. and Schwartz, D. (1999) Rethinking transfer: a simple proposal with multiple implications, in: A. Iran-Nejad and P. D. Pearson (Eds.) Review of Research in Education (24) (Washington DC, American Educational Research Association).

Bruner, J. (1960) The Process of Education. (Cambridge, MA, Harvard University Press).

Bruner, J. (1966) Toward a Theory of Instruction. (Cambridge, MA, Harvard University Press).

Catterall, J. S. (1995) Different Ways of Knowing: Longitudinal Study Second Year Report (Los Angeles, The Galef Institute).

Catterall, J. S. (1999) Chicago Arts Partnerships in Education: Summary Evaluation. Chapter in Fiske, E. B. (ED), Champions of Change: The Impact of the Arts on Human Development, 47-62. (Washington, DC, The National Endowment for the Arts, the MacArthur Foundation, the GE Fund, and the Arts Education Partnership).

Coopersmith, W. (1967) The antecedents of self-esteem (San Francisco, CA, W. H. Freeman).

Eisner, E. W. (2005). Eisner argues "Three Rs Are Essential, but don't forget the A – the Arts, Los Angeles Times, January 3, 2005, p. B7.

Horowitz, R. & Webb-Dempsey, J. (2002) "Promising signs of positive effects: Lessons from the multi-arts studies." In: R. Deasy (Ed.), Critical Links: Learning in the arts and student academic and social development (Washington, DC, Arts Education Partnership).

Johnson D.W. and Johnson R.. (1989) *Cooperation and Competition: Theory and Research*. Edina, MN: Interaction Book Co.

Lave, J. (1988) Cognition in Practice: Mind, Mathematics, and Culture in Everyday Life. (Cambridge, UK, Cambridge University Press).

Lave, J. & Wenger, E. (1990) Situated Learning: Legitimate Peripheral Participation. (Cambridge, UK, Cambridge University Press).

Myers, R. E. and Torrance, E. P. (1964) Torrance Test of Creative Thinking (Boston, Ginn and Company).

Pajares, F. (1996) Self-efficacy beliefs in academic settings, *Review of Educational Research*, 66(4), 543-578.

Raffini, J. (1993) Winners Without Losers: Structures And Strategies For Increasing Student Motivation To Learn (Boston, Allyn and Bacon).

Rogoff, B. (2003) The Cultural Nature of Human Development. (Oxford, Oxford University Press).

Scholz, U., Gutiérrez-Doña, B., Sud, S., & Schwarzer, R. (2002) Is perceived self-efficacy a universal construct? Psychometric findings from 25 countries, European Journal of Psychological Assessment, 18(3) 242-251.

Trusty, J. and Oliva, G. M. (1994) The effect of arts and music education on students' self-concept, Update: *Applications of Research in Music Education* (13)1, 23-28.

Vygotsky, L. (1962) Thought and Language (Cambridge, MA: Harvard University Press).

Vygotsky, L. (1978) Mind in Society (Cambridge, MA: Harvard University Press).

Wu, S. C. (1992) National Education Longitudinal Study of 1988, First Follow-Up: Student Component Data File User's Manual Volume I (U.S. Department of Education).

Arts and Cognition

Ames, C. (1990) *Motivation: what teachers need to know. Teachers College Record* 91/3, pp.409-421.

Anderson, C. (2004) Learning in as-if worlds. cognition in drama education. *Theory Into Practice* 43/4, pp. 281-286.

Bandura, A. (1977) *Social Learning Theory.* (Englewood Cliffs, NJ, Prentice Hall).

Bransford, J. and Schwartz, D. (1999). Rethinking transfer: a simple proposal with multiple implications, Chapter in A. Iran-Nejad and P. D. Pearson (Eds.) *Review of Research in Education, V 24*. (Washington DC, American Educational Research Association).

Bruner, J. (1960) *The Process of Education.* (Cambridge, MA, Harvard University Press).

Bruner, J. (1966) *Toward a Theory of Instruction.* (Cambridge, MA, Harvard University Press).

Bruner, J. (1987) *Actual Minds, Possible Worlds.* Cambridge, MA: Harvard University Press.

Catterall, J. (2002). Research on drama and theatre in education. Chapter in R. Deasy (Ed.) *Critical Links: Learning in the Arts and Student Academic and Social Development.* Washington, DC: National Endowment for the Arts, United States Department of Education, and the Arts Education Partnership.

Catterall, J. S. and Darby, J. T. (1996) Cognition, community, and assessment: toward integrated inquiry on drama in education. Chapter in J. Somers (Ed.) *Drama and Theatre in Education: Contemporary Research.* (North York ON, Canada, Captus University Press).

Fleming, M., Merrill, C. and Tymms, P. (2004) The impact of drama on pupils' language, mathematics, and attitude in two primary schools, *Research in Drama Education* 9/2 pp. 177-197.

Ihanus J & Lipponen L (1997) Jerome Bruner, cultural psychology and narrative thinking. *Psykologia* 32/4 (253-260).

Johnson, D. and Johnson, R. (1980). Integrating handicapped students into the mainstream. *Exceptional Children 47/2*, pp. 90-98.

Johnson, L and O'Neill, C. (Eds.) (1984). *Dorothy Heathcote: Collected Writings on Education and Drama*. (Cheltenham, England, Thornes, Ltd.).

Lave, J. (1988) *Cognition in Practice: Mind, Mathematics, and Culture in Everyday Life*. (Cambridge, UK, Cambridge University Press).

Lave, J. & Wenger, E. (1990) *Situated Learning: Legitimate Peripheral Participation*. (Cambridge, UK: Cambridge University Press).

Rogoff, B. (2003) *The Cultural Nature of Human Development*. (Oxford, Oxford University Press).

Somers, J. (Ed.) (1996) *Drama and Theatre in Education: Contemporary Research*. (North York ON, Canada: Captus University Press.)

United States Department of Education (1989). National Education Longitudinal Study of 1988. (Contact Jeffrey Owings, National Center for Education Statistics, Washington DC.)

Vygotsky, L. (1962) *Thought and Language*. (Cambridge, MA: Harvard University Press).

Vygotsky, L. (1978). *Mind in Society*. (Cambridge, MA: Harvard University Press).

Music and Cognition

Bahr, N., & Christensen, C.A. (2000). Inter-domain transfer between mathematical skill and musicianship. *Journal of Structural Learning and Intelligent Systems, 14*, 187-197.

Bhattacharya, J., & Petsche, H. (2001). Universality in the brain while listening to music. *Proceedings of the Royal Society of London, 268*, 2423-2433.

Bhattacharya, J., Petsche, H., Feldmann, U., & Rescher, B. (2001). EEG gamma band phase synchronization between posterior and frontal cortex during mental rotation in humans. *Neuroscience Letters, 311*, 29-32.

Bilhartz, T.D., Bruhn, R.A., & Olson, J.E. (2000). The effects of early music training on child cognitive development. *Journal of Applied Developmental Psychology, 20*, 615-636.

Brochard, R., Dufour, A., & Després, O. (2004). Effect of musical expertise on visuospatial abilities: Evidence from reaction times and mental imagery. *Brain and Cognition, 54,* 103-109.

Byrnes, J.P. (1996). *Cognitive development and learning in instructional contexts.* Boston: Allyn and Bacon.

Catterall, J. S. and Rauscher, F. "Unpacking the impact of music on intelligence." Chapter in *Neurosciences and Music Pedagogy.* W. Gruhn (Ed.). Hauppage, NY: Nova Science Publishers (2007).

Chan, A.S., Ho, Y.C., & Cheung, M.C. (1998). Music training improves verbal memory. *Nature, 396,* 128.

Costa-Giomi, E. (1999). The effects of three years of piano instruction on children's cognitive development. *Journal of Research in Music Education, 47,* 198-212.

Coward, L. A. 1990. Pattern Thinking. Westbrook, CT: Greenwood Press.

Cranberg, L.D., & Albert, M.L. (1988). The chess mind. In K.L. Obler & D. Fein (Eds.), *The exceptional brain* (pp. 156-190). New York: The Guilford Press.

Crncec, R., Wilson, S.J., & Prior, M. (2006). No evidence for the Mozart effect in children. *Music Perception, 23,* 305-317.

Dong, Y., Fukuyama, H., Honda, M., Okada, T., Hanakawa, T., Nakamura, K. et al. (1995). Essential role of the right superior parietal cortex in Japanese kana mirror reading: an fMRI study. *Brain, 123,* 790-799.

Fuster, J.M. (1995). Temporal processing. *Annals of the New York Academy of Sciences, 769,* 173-181.

Gardiner, M.F., Fox, A., Knowles, F., & Jeffrey, D. (1996) Learning improved by arts training. *Nature, 381,* 284.

Gardner, M.F. (1996). *Test of auditory-perceptual skills.* Hydesville, CA: Psychological and Educational Publications.

Graziano, A.B., Peterson, M., & Shaw, G.L. (1999). Enhanced learning of proportional math through music training and spatial-temporal training. *Neurological Research, 21,* 139-152.

Gromko, J.E., & Poorman, A.S. (1998). The effect of music training on preschoolers' spatial-temporal task performance. *Journal of Research in Music Education, 46,* 173-181.

Hammill, D.D., Pearson, N.A., & Voress, J.K. (1993). *Developmental test of visual perception.* Austin, TX: Pro-ed.

Hassler, M., & Birbaumer, N. (1988). Handedness, musical

abilities and dichaptic and dichotic performance in adolescents: A longitudinal study. *Developmental Neuropsychology, 4,* 129-145.

Hassler, M., Birbaumer, N., & Feil, A. (1985). Musical talent and visual-spatial abilities: A longitudinal study. *Psychology of Music, 13,* 99-113.

Hassler, M., Birbaumer, N., & Feil, A. (1987). Musical talent and visual-spatial ability: Onset o puberty. *Psychology of Music,* 15, 141-151.

Hassler, M., & Feil, A. (1986). A study of the relationship of composition/improvisation to selected personal variables. *Bulletin of the Council for Research in Music Education, 87,* 26-34.

Hassler, M., Nieschlag, E., & De LaMotte, D. (1990). Creative musical talent, cognitive functioning, and gender: Psychological aspects. *Music Perception, 8,* 35-48.

Hebb, D.O. (1949). The organization of behavior: A neuropsychological theory. New York: Wiley.

Hetland, L. (2000). Learning to make music enhances spatial reasoning. *Journal of Aesthetic Education, 34,* 179-238.

Ho, Y.C., Cheung, M.C., & Chan, A.S. (2003). Music training improves verbal but not visual memory: Cross sectional and longitudinal explorations in children. *Neuropsychology, 17,* 439-450.

Hui, K. (2006). Mozart effect in preschool children? *Early Childhood Development and Care, 176,* 411-419.

Hurwitz, I., Wolff, P.H., Bortnick, B.D., & Kokas, K. (1975). Nonmusical effects of the Kodàly music curriculum in primary grade children. *Journal of Learning Disabilities, 8,* 167-174.

Ivanov, V.K., & Geake, J.G. (2003). The Mozart effect and primary school children. *Psychology of Music, 31,* 405-413.

Jausovec, N., & Habe, K. (2004). The influence of auditory background stimulation (Mozart's sonata K. 448) on visual brain activity. *International Journal of Psychophysics, 51,*261-271.

Jausovec, N., & Habe, K. (2005). The influence of Mozart's sonata K. 448 on brain activity during the performance of spatial rotation and numerical tasks. *Brain Topography, 17,* 207-218.

Jeannerod. M., Decety, J., Michel, F. (1994). Impairment of grasping movements following a bilateral posterior parietal lesion. *Neuropsychologia, 32,* 369-380.

Karma, K. (1982). Musical, spatial, and verbal abilities: A progress report. *Psychology of Music,* Special Issue, 69-71.

Kaufman, A.S., & Kaufman, N.L. (1983). *Kaufman assessment battery for children*. Circle Pines, MN: American Guidance Service.

Kilgour, A.R., Jakobson, L.S., & Cuddy, L.L. (2000). Music training and rate of presentations as mediator of text and son recall. *Memory and Cognition, 28*, 700-710.

Lamb, S.J., & Gregory, A.H. (1993). The relationship between music and reading in beginning readers. *Educational Psychology, 13*, 19-27.

McKelvie, P., & Low, J. (2002). Listening to Mozart does not improve children's spatial ability: Final curtains for the Mozart effect. *British Journal of Developmental Psychology, 20*, 241-258.

Orsmond, G.I., & Miller, L.K. (1995). Correlates of musical improvisations in children with disabilities. *Journal of Music Therapy, 32*, 152-166.

Orsmond, G.I., & Miller, L.K. (1999). Cognitive, musical and environmental correlates of early music instruction. *Psychology of Music, 27*, 18-37.0

Perkins, D.N., & Salomon, G. (1989). Are cognitive skills context-bound? *Educational Researcher, 18*, 16-25.

Rauscher, F.H. (2002). Mozart and the mind: Factual and fictional effects of musical enrichment. In J. Aronson (Ed.), *Improving academic achievement: Impact of psychological factors on education* (pp. 269-278). New York: Academic Press.

Rauscher, F.H., & Hinton S.C. (in press). The Mozart effect: Music listening is not music instruction. *Educational Psychologist*.

Rauscher, F.H., LeMieux, M., & Hinton, S.C. (2005, August). *Selective effects of music instruction on cognitive performance of at-risk children*. Paper presented at the bi-annual meeting of the European Conference on Developmental Psychology, Tenerife, Canary Islands.

Rauscher, F.H., LeMieux, M.M., & Hinton, S.C. (2006, August). *Quality piano instruction affects at-risk elementary school children's cognitive abilities and self-esteem*. Paper presented at the Ninth International Conference on Music Perception and Cognition, Bologna, Italy.

Rauscher, F.H., & Shaw, G.L. (1998). Key components of the "Mozart Effect." *Perceptual and Motor Skills, 86*, 835-841.

Rauscher, F.H., Shaw, G.L., & Ky, K.N. (1993). Music and spatial task performance. *Nature, 365*, 611.

Rauscher, F.H., Shaw, G.L., Levine, L.J., Wright, E.L., Dennis, W.R., & Newcomb, R. (1997). Music training causes long-term enhancement of preschool children's spatial-temporal reasoning abilities. *Neurological Research, 19*, 1-8.

Rauscher, F.H., & Zupan, M.A.(2000). Classroom keyboard instruction improves kindergarten children's spatial-temporal performance: A field experiment. *Early Childhood Research Quarterly, 15*, 215-228.

Raven, J.C. (1956). *Coloured progressive matrices.* London: H.K. Lewis.

Raven, J. C. (1986). *Standard progressive matrices.* San Antonio, TX: The Psychological Corporation.

Sarnthein, J., von Stein, A., Rappelsberger, P., Petsche, H., Rauscher, F.H., & Shaw, G.L. (1997). Persistent patterns of brain activity: an EEG coherence study of the positive effect of music on spatial-temporal reasoning. Neurological Research, 19, 107-116.

Scandura, J.M. (1984). Structural (cognitive task) analysis: A method for analyzing content: Part 2. Toward precision, objectivity and systematization. *Journal of Structural Learning, 8,* 1-28.

Schellenberg, E. G. (2005). Music and cognitive abilities. *Current Directions in Psychological Science,* 14, 322-325.

Schellenberg, E.G. (2004). Music lessons enhance IQ. *Psychological Science, 15,* 511-514.

Schellenberg, E. G., & Hallam, S. (2005). Music listening and cognitive abilities in 10- and 11-year-olds: The Blur effect. *Annals of the New York Academy of Sciences,* 1060, 202-209.

Schellenberg, E. G., Nakata, T., Hunter, P. G., & Tamoto, S. (in press).

Exposure to music and cognitive performance: Tests of children and adults. *Psychology of Music.*

Thorndike, E.L. (1913). *Educational psychology.* New York: Columbia University Press.

Thorndike, E.L., Hagen, E.P., & Sattler, J.M. (1986). *The Stanford-Binet intelligence scale* (4th ed.). Chicago: Riverside.

Vaughn, K. (2000). Music and mathematics: Modest support for the oft-claimed relationship. *Journal of Aesthetic Education, 34,* 149-166.

Wechsler, D. (1989). *Wechsler preschool and primary scale of intelligence-revised.* San Antonio, TX: The Psychological Corporation.

Wechsler, D. (1991). *Wechsler intelligence scale for children —third edition.* San Antonio, TX: Psychological Corporation.

Zafranas, N. (2004). Piano keyboard training and the spatial-temporal development of young children attending kindergarten in Greece. *Early Childhood Development and Care, 174,* 199-211.

Doing Well and Doing Good by Doing Art

c2009 I-Group Books

Los Angeles, CA 90290

www.i-groupbooks@co.uk

See this website for single or quantity book orders with discounted or free shipping.

igroupbooks@gmail.com

Author contact:

jamesc@gseis.ucla.edu

2716216R00106

Made in the USA
San Bernardino, CA
27 May 2013